Grade 6

KUMON MATH WORKBOOKS

Fractions

Table of Contents

Addition of Fractions

Level ☆

Date / /

Name

Score

/100

---

1 **Add.**

5 points per question

(1) $\dfrac{3}{5}+\dfrac{1}{5}=\dfrac{4}{5}$

(2) $\dfrac{3}{5}+\dfrac{2}{5}=\dfrac{5}{5}=1$

(3) $\dfrac{4}{7}+\dfrac{2}{7}=\dfrac{6}{7}$

(4) $\dfrac{4}{7}+\dfrac{5}{7}=\dfrac{9}{7}=1\dfrac{2}{7}$

(5) $2+\dfrac{4}{5}=$

(6) $1\dfrac{2}{3}+2=$

(7) $2\dfrac{3}{7}+\dfrac{2}{7}=$

(8) $\dfrac{7}{8}+1\dfrac{1}{8}=$

(9) $1\dfrac{5}{9}+1\dfrac{2}{9}=$

(10) $1\dfrac{6}{11}+2\dfrac{5}{11}=$

---

2   © Kumon Publishing Co., Ltd.

2 **Add.**

(1) $\frac{3}{7} + \frac{2}{7} = \frac{6}{7}$

(2) $\frac{7}{9} + \frac{4}{9} =$

(3) $2\frac{2}{5} + \frac{1}{5} =$

(4) $\frac{3}{7} + 1\frac{6}{7} =$

(5) $1\frac{3}{5} + 2\frac{4}{5} =$

(6) $\frac{4}{9} + \frac{4}{9} = \frac{8}{9}$

(7) $2 + 2\frac{3}{7} =$
     $\frac{2}{1} + \frac{17}{7} =$

(8) $2\frac{1}{6} + 1\frac{5}{6} =$

(9) $1\frac{4}{7} + 2\frac{5}{7} =$

(10) $\frac{3}{11} + 3\frac{9}{11} =$

Do you remember how to add your fractions?

3

2 Subtraction of Fractions

Date / /

Name

Score

/100

1 Subtract.

5 points per question

(1) $\dfrac{4}{5} - \dfrac{1}{5} =$

(6) $3\dfrac{2}{5} - 2 =$

(2) $\dfrac{6}{7} - \dfrac{2}{7} =$

(7) $2\dfrac{6}{7} - 1\dfrac{3}{7} =$

(3) $1 - \dfrac{1}{4} =$

(8) $2 - \dfrac{3}{5} =$

(4) $\dfrac{6}{5} - \dfrac{2}{5} =$

(9) $4 - 1\dfrac{5}{9} =$

(5) $2\dfrac{4}{7} - \dfrac{2}{7} =$

(10) $3\dfrac{2}{5} - \dfrac{4}{5} =$

2 **Subtract.**

5 points per question

(1) $1 - \dfrac{5}{6} =$

(2) $3 - 1\dfrac{2}{5} =$

(3) $\dfrac{8}{9} - \dfrac{3}{9} =$

(4) $\dfrac{9}{7} - \dfrac{4}{7} =$

(5) $2\dfrac{8}{11} - \dfrac{5}{11} =$

(6) $2 - \dfrac{3}{8} =$

(7) $\dfrac{5}{7} - \dfrac{4}{7} =$

(8) $3\dfrac{1}{5} - 1\dfrac{2}{5} =$

(9) $4\dfrac{10}{11} - 3\dfrac{6}{11} =$

(10) $2\dfrac{2}{9} - 1\dfrac{7}{9} =$

Can you subtract your fractions, too?
Good job.

© Kumon Publishing Co., Ltd.   5

3 Mixed Review

Level

Date / /

Name

Score

/100

1 **Add.**

5 points per question

(1) $\dfrac{2}{5} + \dfrac{4}{5} =$

(2) $\dfrac{2}{7} + \dfrac{3}{7} =$

(3) $2\dfrac{5}{6} + 1 =$

(4) $1\dfrac{1}{9} + 2\dfrac{4}{9} =$

(5) $\dfrac{8}{11} + 1\dfrac{4}{11} =$

(6) $3 + \dfrac{3}{8} =$

(7) $\dfrac{5}{9} + \dfrac{4}{9} =$

(8) $\dfrac{6}{7} + 2\dfrac{3}{7} =$

(9) $1\dfrac{3}{11} + 3\dfrac{7}{11} =$

(10) $2\dfrac{7}{9} + 1\dfrac{4}{9} =$

② **Subtract.**

(1) $\dfrac{8}{7} - \dfrac{3}{7} =$

(2) $1 - \dfrac{4}{9} =$

(3) $\dfrac{4}{5} - \dfrac{4}{5} =$

(4) $1\dfrac{6}{11} - \dfrac{3}{11} =$

(5) $2\dfrac{1}{7} - 1\dfrac{5}{7} =$

(6) $2 - \dfrac{1}{3} =$

(7) $\dfrac{8}{11} - \dfrac{3}{11} =$

(8) $2\dfrac{5}{7} - 1\dfrac{2}{7} =$

(9) $3 - 2\dfrac{4}{9} =$

(10) $3\dfrac{2}{11} - 1\dfrac{6}{11} =$

All right! Are you ready for something new?

4 Reduction

Date   /   /

Name

Level ☆☆

Score

/100

Don't forget!

$$\frac{2}{8} = \frac{1}{4} \qquad \frac{10}{12} = \frac{5}{6} \qquad \text{Divide both the denominator and the numerator by 2.}$$

Reduction is the process in which a fraction is simplified by dividing the denominator and numerator by the same number.

---

1 **Reduce by dividing the denominator and the numerator by 2.**

2 points per question

(1) $\dfrac{2}{6} = \dfrac{\square}{3}$

(2) $\dfrac{6}{8} = \dfrac{3}{\square}$

(3) $\dfrac{2}{4} =$

(4) $\dfrac{4}{6} =$

(5) $\dfrac{8}{10} =$

(6) $\dfrac{4}{14} =$

(7) $\dfrac{6}{16} =$

(8) $\dfrac{10}{18} =$

(9) $\dfrac{18}{20} =$

(10) $\dfrac{16}{26} =$

2 **Reduce by dividing the denominator and the numerator by 3.**

2 points per question

Example $\dfrac{6}{9} = \dfrac{2}{3} \qquad \dfrac{15}{18} = \dfrac{5}{6}$

(1) $\dfrac{3}{6} =$

(2) $\dfrac{3}{9} =$

(3) $\dfrac{9}{12} =$

(4) $\dfrac{6}{15} =$

(5) $\dfrac{9}{15} =$

(6) $\dfrac{12}{15} =$

(7) $\dfrac{9}{21} =$

(8) $\dfrac{21}{24} =$

(9) $\dfrac{12}{27} =$

(10) $\dfrac{24}{27} =$

3 **Reduce by dividing the denominator and the numerator by either 2 or 3.**

(1) $\dfrac{2}{6} =$

(2) $\dfrac{3}{6} =$

(3) $\dfrac{4}{6} =$

(4) $\dfrac{6}{8} =$

(5) $\dfrac{6}{10} =$

(6) $\dfrac{10}{12} =$

(7) $\dfrac{6}{15} =$

(8) $\dfrac{14}{16} =$

(9) $\dfrac{10}{18} =$

(10) $\dfrac{15}{18} =$

(11) $\dfrac{3}{21} =$

(12) $\dfrac{18}{21} =$

(13) $\dfrac{8}{22} =$

(14) $\dfrac{10}{24} =$

(15) $\dfrac{15}{24} =$

(16) $\dfrac{6}{26} =$

(17) $\dfrac{6}{27} =$

(18) $\dfrac{8}{30} =$

(19) $\dfrac{9}{30} =$

(20) $\dfrac{21}{30} =$

Nice work! It's not so bad, right?

5 Reduction

Date   /   /

Name

1 Reduce. (Try using either 2 or 5.)

2 points per question

(1) $\dfrac{4}{6} =$

(2) $\dfrac{5}{10} =$

(3) $\dfrac{10}{12} =$

(4) $\dfrac{10}{15} =$

(5) $\dfrac{5}{20} =$

(6) $\dfrac{14}{24} =$

(7) $\dfrac{15}{25} =$

(8) $\dfrac{14}{30} =$

(9) $\dfrac{25}{30} =$

(10) $\dfrac{35}{40} =$

2 Reduce. (Try using either 3 or 5.)

3 points per question

(1) $\dfrac{3}{6} =$

(2) $\dfrac{6}{9} =$

(3) $\dfrac{5}{15} =$

(4) $\dfrac{15}{20} =$

(5) $\dfrac{3}{21} =$

(6) $\dfrac{12}{21} =$

(7) $\dfrac{5}{25} =$

(8) $\dfrac{10}{25} =$

(9) $\dfrac{20}{25} =$

(10) $\dfrac{21}{27} =$

3 Reduce. (Try using either 2 or 7.)

2 points per question

(1) $\dfrac{6}{8} =$

(2) $\dfrac{4}{10} =$

(3) $\dfrac{10}{12} =$

(4) $\dfrac{6}{14} =$

(5) $\dfrac{7}{14} =$

(6) $\dfrac{14}{18} =$

(7) $\dfrac{14}{21} =$

(8) $\dfrac{16}{22} =$

(9) $\dfrac{21}{28} =$

(10) $\dfrac{28}{35} =$

4 Reduce. (Try using either 3 or 7.)

3 points per question

(1) $\dfrac{9}{15} =$

(2) $\dfrac{6}{21} =$

(3) $\dfrac{7}{21} =$

(4) $\dfrac{15}{21} =$

(5) $\dfrac{9}{24} =$

(6) $\dfrac{21}{24} =$

(7) $\dfrac{7}{28} =$

(8) $\dfrac{14}{35} =$

(9) $\dfrac{21}{35} =$

(10) $\dfrac{35}{42} =$

Well done! Now, let's check your score.

6 Reduction

Date / /

Name

Level ☆☆

Score
/100

1 Reduce. (Try using either 5 or 7.)

2 points per question

(1) $\dfrac{7}{14} = \dfrac{1}{2}$

(5) $\dfrac{7}{35} = \dfrac{2}{7}$

(9) $\dfrac{28}{35} =$

(2) $\dfrac{10}{25} =$

(6) $\dfrac{14}{35} =$

(10) $\dfrac{35}{42} =$

(3) $\dfrac{7}{28} =$

(7) $\dfrac{15}{35} =$

(4) $\dfrac{5}{35} =$

(8) $\dfrac{25}{35} =$

2 Reduce.

3 points per question

(1) $\dfrac{6}{10} =$

(5) $\dfrac{28}{34} =$

(9) $\dfrac{20}{45} =$

(2) $\dfrac{14}{22} =$

(6) $\dfrac{2}{38} =$

(10) $\dfrac{14}{49} =$

(3) $\dfrac{21}{24} =$

(7) $\dfrac{27}{39} =$

(4) $\dfrac{22}{26} =$

(8) $\dfrac{15}{40} =$

3 **Reduce.**

2 points per question

(1) $\dfrac{8}{12} = \dfrac{\square}{3}$

(2) $\dfrac{4}{8} =$

(3) $\dfrac{4}{12} =$

(4) $\dfrac{12}{16} =$

(5) $\dfrac{16}{20} =$

(6) $\dfrac{6}{18} = \dfrac{1}{\square}$

(7) $\dfrac{6}{12} =$

(8) $\dfrac{12}{18} =$

(9) $\dfrac{18}{24} =$

(10) $\dfrac{18}{30} =$

4 **Reduce. (You may want to reduce more than once.)**

3 points per question

Example $\quad \dfrac{12}{16} = \dfrac{6}{8} = \dfrac{3}{4} \qquad \dfrac{12}{16} = \dfrac{3}{4}$

(1) $\dfrac{4}{16} =$

(2) $\dfrac{8}{16} =$

(3) $\dfrac{16}{20} =$

(4) $\dfrac{8}{24} =$

(5) $\dfrac{16}{24} =$

(6) $\dfrac{8}{28} =$

(7) $\dfrac{8}{32} =$

(8) $\dfrac{20}{32} =$

(9) $\dfrac{24}{32} =$

(10) $\dfrac{16}{36} =$

You're doing really well! Let's keep going!

7 **Reduction**

Level

Date / /

Name

Score

/100

1 **Reduce. (Try to reduce as much as possible in one try.)**

2 points per question

(1) $\dfrac{12}{16} =$

(2) $\dfrac{6}{18} =$

(3) $\dfrac{16}{28} =$

(4) $\dfrac{24}{30} =$

(5) $\dfrac{27}{36} =$

(6) $\dfrac{18}{45} =$

(7) $\dfrac{36}{45} =$

(8) $\dfrac{10}{20} =$

(9) $\dfrac{10}{30} =$

(10) $\dfrac{20}{30} =$

(11) $\dfrac{10}{40} =$

(12) $\dfrac{30}{40} =$

(13) $\dfrac{28}{40} =$

(14) $\dfrac{40}{48} =$

(15) $\dfrac{35}{50} =$

(16) $\dfrac{40}{50} =$

(17) $\dfrac{9}{54} =$

(18) $\dfrac{24}{54} =$

(19) $\dfrac{16}{56} =$

(20) $\dfrac{25}{60} =$

2 **Reduce. (Try to reduce as much as possible in one try.)** 3 points per question

(1) $\dfrac{3}{12}=$

(2) $\dfrac{4}{12}=$

(3) $\dfrac{8}{24}=$

(4) $\dfrac{12}{24}=$

(5) $\dfrac{9}{27}=$

(6) $\dfrac{18}{27}=$

(7) $\dfrac{9}{36}=$

(8) $\dfrac{12}{36}=$

(9) $\dfrac{14}{42}=$

(10) $\dfrac{28}{42}=$

(11) $\dfrac{35}{49}=$

(12) $\dfrac{12}{54}=$

(13) $\dfrac{18}{54}=$

(14) $\dfrac{8}{56}=$

(15) $\dfrac{14}{56}=$

(16) $\dfrac{12}{60}=$

(17) $\dfrac{15}{60}=$

(18) $\dfrac{20}{60}=$

(19) $\dfrac{30}{60}=$

(20) $\dfrac{40}{60}=$

Don't worry if you have to reduce twice.
You'll get the hang of it!

Reduction

Don't forget!

12 can be evenly divided by 4. 12 can also be evenly divided by 6. (There is no remainder.)

12 can't be evenly divided by 5. (There is a remainder.)

This means that 4 and 6 are **factors** of 12.

---

1 Write the appropriate number in each box below.

5 points per question

(1) The factors of 12 are ... 1, 2, 3, 4, ☐, 12

(2) The factors of 18 are ... 1, 2, 3, 6, ☐, 18

(3) The common factors of 12 and 18 are ... 1, 2, 3, ☐

> **Don't forget!**
> The factors that two integers have in common are called **common factors**.

2 Write the appropriate number in each box below.

5 points per question

(1) The factors of 20 are ... 1, 2, 4, ☐, 10, 20,

(2) The factors of 30 are ... 1, 2, 3, 5, ☐, 10, 15, 30

(3) The common factors of 20 and 30 are ... 1, 2, 5, ☐

3 Write the appropriate number in each box below.

5 points per question

(1) The largest number in the common factors of 12 and 18 is ☐.

(2) The largest number in the common factors of 20 and 30 is ☐.

> **Don't forget!**
> Among the common factors, the largest factor that two integers have in common is called the **greatest common factor (GCF)**.

4 Write the greatest common factor in each box below.

5 points per question

Example (12, 18) → ☐ 6

(1) (8, 12) → ☐

(2) (12, 30) → ☐

(3) (18, 30) → ☐

(4) (24, 40) → ☐

5 Find the greatest common factor (GCF). Then reduce the fraction by the GCF.

4 points per question

Example (12, 18) → GCF: 6 $\frac{12}{18}=\frac{2}{3}$

(1) (12, 20) → ☐ $\frac{12}{20}=$

(2) (20, 24) → ☐ $\frac{20}{24}=$

(3) (18, 24) → ☐ $\frac{18}{24}=$

(4) (12, 30) → ☐ $\frac{12}{30}=$

(5) (15, 30) → ☐ $\frac{15}{30}=$

(6) (18, 27) → ☐ $\frac{18}{27}=$

(7) (24, 32) → ☐ $\frac{24}{32}=$

(8) (27, 36) → ☐ $\frac{27}{36}=$

(9) (36, 48) → ☐ $\frac{36}{48}=$

(10) (45, 60) → ☐ $\frac{45}{60}=$

Getting a handle on the greatest common factor? Good job!

Date / /

Name

Level ★★★

Score / 100

Don't forget!

You can use the method shown on the right to find the GCF.

Example (16, 20) → GCF 4

Divide using the simple common factors.

$\underset{2)}{}$ 16, 20 ← Divide by 2.
$2)$ 8, 10 ← Divide by 2.
 4, 5 ← You can't divide these numbers any more.

$2 \times 2 = \boxed{4}$ ← GCF

---

1 Find the greatest common factor.

4 points per question

(1) (18, 30) → ☐

(2) (20, 30) → ☐

(3) (48, 54) → ☐

(4) (30, 60) → ☐

(5) (48, 60) → ☐

(6) (14, 35) → ☐

(7) (24, 40) → ☐

(8) (27, 54) → ☐

(9) (24, 60) → ☐

(10) (36, 54) → ☐

(1)
$2)$ 18, 30 ← Divide by 2.
$3)$ 9, 15 ← Divide by 3.
 3, 5 ← You can't divide these numbers any more.

$2 \times 3 = \boxed{}$ ← GCF

2 **Reduce. (Try to use the GCF.)**

3 points per question

(1) $\dfrac{4}{12}=$

(2) $\dfrac{4}{16}=$

(3) $\dfrac{12}{16}=$

(4) $\dfrac{6}{18}=$

(5) $\dfrac{12}{18}=$

(6) $\dfrac{14}{21}=$

(7) $\dfrac{12}{24}=$

(8) $\dfrac{16}{28}=$

(9) $\dfrac{24}{30}=$

(10) $\dfrac{25}{30}=$

(11) $\dfrac{12}{36}=$

(12) $\dfrac{27}{36}=$

(13) $\dfrac{16}{40}=$

(14) $\dfrac{12}{42}=$

(15) $\dfrac{14}{42}=$

(16) $\dfrac{20}{48}=$

(17) $\dfrac{33}{51}=$

(18) $\dfrac{36}{54}=$

(19) $\dfrac{40}{64}=$

(20) $\dfrac{18}{66}=$

Did you solve all of the problems?
Let's check your answers.

Level ★★

Score   /100

1 **Calculate using the example as a guide.**

3 points per question

Example $\dfrac{1}{3} = \dfrac{\boxed{2}}{6}$ $\dfrac{1}{5} = \dfrac{\boxed{3}}{15}$ $\dfrac{2}{7} = \dfrac{\boxed{16}}{56}$

(1) $\dfrac{1}{2} = \dfrac{\square}{6}$

(2) $\dfrac{1}{3} = \dfrac{\square}{12}$

(3) $\dfrac{1}{4} = \dfrac{\square}{8}$

(4) $\dfrac{1}{5} = \dfrac{\square}{15}$

(5) $\dfrac{2}{5} = \dfrac{\square}{20}$

(6) $\dfrac{1}{7} = \dfrac{\square}{35}$

(7) $\dfrac{3}{7} = \dfrac{\square}{42}$

(8) $\dfrac{5}{8} = \dfrac{\square}{24}$

(9) $\dfrac{2}{9} = \dfrac{\square}{18}$

(10) $\dfrac{5}{9} = \dfrac{\square}{27}$

(11) $\dfrac{1}{2} = \dfrac{}{8}$

(12) $\dfrac{2}{3} = \dfrac{}{21}$

(13) $\dfrac{3}{4} = \dfrac{}{28}$

(14) $\dfrac{3}{5} = \dfrac{}{40}$

(15) $\dfrac{2}{6} = \dfrac{}{36}$

(16) $\dfrac{4}{7} = \dfrac{}{56}$

(17) $\dfrac{3}{8} = \dfrac{}{80}$

(18) $\dfrac{7}{8} = \dfrac{}{72}$

(19) $\dfrac{1}{9} = \dfrac{}{81}$

(20) $\dfrac{4}{9} = \dfrac{}{63}$

2 **Add.**

Example

$$\frac{1}{8} + \frac{1}{4} = \frac{1}{8} + \frac{2}{8}$$

$$= \frac{3}{8}$$

When adding fractions with unlike denominators, you need to first make the denominators equal.

(1) $\dfrac{3}{8} + \dfrac{1}{4} = \dfrac{3}{8} + \dfrac{\square}{8}$

$=$

(2) $\dfrac{5}{8} + \dfrac{1}{4} = \dfrac{\square}{8} + \dfrac{\square}{8}$

$=$

(3) $\dfrac{1}{9} + \dfrac{1}{3} = \dfrac{1}{9} + \dfrac{\square}{9}$

$=$

(4) $\dfrac{4}{9} + \dfrac{1}{3} = \dfrac{}{9} + \dfrac{}{9}$

$=$

(5) $\dfrac{1}{8} + \dfrac{1}{2} = \dfrac{}{8} + \dfrac{}{8}$

$=$

(6) $\dfrac{1}{6} + \dfrac{2}{3} = \dfrac{1}{6} + \dfrac{}{6}$

$=$

(7) $\dfrac{1}{10} + \dfrac{1}{5} = \dfrac{}{10} + \dfrac{}{10}$

$=$

(8) $\dfrac{2}{5} + \dfrac{3}{10} =$

(9) $\dfrac{1}{12} + \dfrac{1}{3} = \dfrac{}{12} + \dfrac{}{12}$

$=$

(10) $\dfrac{1}{3} + \dfrac{7}{12} =$

This is called "finding the lowest common denominator!" Good job!

1 **Add.**

5 points per question

(1) $\dfrac{1}{12}+\dfrac{1}{6}=\dfrac{\square}{12}+\dfrac{\square}{12}$

$=\dfrac{\square}{12}=\dfrac{\square}{4}$

(2) $\dfrac{7}{12}+\dfrac{1}{6}=$

(3) $\dfrac{1}{12}+\dfrac{1}{4}=\dfrac{}{12}+\dfrac{}{12}$

(4) $\dfrac{5}{12}+\dfrac{1}{4}=$

(5) $\dfrac{1}{4}+\dfrac{7}{12}=$

(6) $\dfrac{1}{18}+\dfrac{1}{6}=\dfrac{}{18}+\dfrac{}{18}$

$=$

(7) $\dfrac{1}{6}+\dfrac{5}{18}=$

(8) $\dfrac{1}{6}+\dfrac{7}{18}=$

(9) $\dfrac{1}{9}+\dfrac{1}{18}=\dfrac{}{18}+\dfrac{}{18}$

$=$

(10) $\dfrac{1}{18}+\dfrac{4}{9}=$

2 **Add.**

(1) $\dfrac{1}{2}+\dfrac{5}{8}=\dfrac{\square}{8}+\dfrac{\square}{8}$

$\qquad\qquad =\dfrac{\square}{8}=1\dfrac{\square}{8}$

(2) $\dfrac{2}{3}+\dfrac{4}{9}=$

(3) $\dfrac{1}{3}+\dfrac{5}{6}=$

(4) $\dfrac{1}{4}+\dfrac{7}{8}=$

(5) $\dfrac{3}{10}+\dfrac{4}{5}=$

(6) $\dfrac{5}{6}+\dfrac{5}{24}=\dfrac{}{24}+\dfrac{}{24}$

$\qquad\qquad =$

(7) $\dfrac{1}{2}+\dfrac{3}{4}=$

(8) $\dfrac{7}{8}+\dfrac{1}{2}=$

(9) $\dfrac{7}{9}+\dfrac{2}{3}=$

(10) $\dfrac{3}{4}+\dfrac{5}{8}=$

Are you getting the hang of it?
Now we'll try something a little different.

Addition of Fractions

Level ★★

Date ___/___/___

Name _____

Score ___/100

1 Write the multiples of 6 in ascending order.

5 points for completion

6, 12, 18, ☐, ☐, ☐, ☐, ☐, ☐

2 Write the multiples of 8 in ascending order.

5 points for completion

8, 16, ☐, ☐, ☐, ☐, ☐

3 Write the multiples of 9 in ascending order.

5 points for completion

9, ☐, ☐, ☐, ☐, ☐

4 Write the numbers which are multiples of both 6 and 8 in ascending order.

5 points for completion

☐, ☐, ☐, ☐

> **Don't forget!**
> The numbers that are multiples of both 6 and 8 are called the **common multiples**.

5 Write the common multiples of 6 and 9 in ascending order.

5 points for completion

☐, ☐, ☐, ☐

> **Don't forget!**
> The smallest common multiple is called **the least common multiple (LCM)**.

6 Write the common multiples of 4 and 6 in ascending order.

5 points for completion

☐, ☐, ☐, ☐

7 Write the appropriate number in each box below.

5 points per question

(1) The smallest number in the common multiples of 6 and 9 is … ☐

(2) The smallest number in the common multiples of 4 and 6 is … ☐

8 Find the least common multiple.

5 points per question

Example (6, 9) → ☐ 18

(1) (6, 8) → ☐

(2) (9, 12) → ☐

9 Find the least common multiple.

5 points per question

(1) (4 , 6) → ☐

(3) (9 , 15) → ☐

(2) (6 , 10) → ☐

(4) (4 , 10) → ☐

10 Write the appropriate numbers in the boxes below in order to add the fractions.

5 points per question

(1) $\dfrac{1}{6} + \dfrac{1}{9}$

The least common multiple of 6 and 9 is 18.

$$\frac{1}{6} = \frac{\Box}{18}, \quad \frac{1}{9} = \frac{\Box}{18}$$

$$\frac{1}{6} + \frac{1}{9} = \frac{\Box}{18} + \frac{\Box}{18}$$

$$= \frac{\Box}{18}$$

(2) $\dfrac{1}{6} + \dfrac{4}{9} = \dfrac{\Box}{18} + \dfrac{\Box}{18}$

$$= \frac{\Box}{18}$$

11 Write the appropriate numbers in the boxes below in order to add the fractions.

5 points per question

(1) The least common multiple of 6 and 8 is ☐ .

(2) $\dfrac{1}{6} + \dfrac{1}{8} = \dfrac{\Box}{24} + \dfrac{\Box}{24}$

$$= \frac{\Box}{24}$$

(3) $\dfrac{1}{6} + \dfrac{5}{8} = \dfrac{\Box}{\Box} + \dfrac{\Box}{\Box}$

$$= \frac{\Box}{\Box}$$

(4) $\dfrac{5}{6} + \dfrac{1}{8} = \Box$

$$= \Box$$

If you have a hard time with a problem, just try it again!

13 Addition of Fractions

Level ★★

Date   /   /

Name

Score
        /100

1 Find the least common multiple, and then add the fractions.

8 points per question

Example (6 , 8) → LCM 24

$$\frac{1}{6}+\frac{1}{8}=\frac{4}{24}+\frac{3}{24}$$

$$=\frac{7}{24}$$

If you can't find the LCM easily, try doing the multiples of the larger denominator until you find one that works. For example, for 8 and 10, try 10, 20, 30…

(1) (4 , 6) → ☐

$$\frac{1}{4}+\frac{1}{6}=\frac{\square}{12}+\frac{\square}{12}$$

$$=$$

(2) (4 , 10) → ☐

$$\frac{1}{4}+\frac{3}{10}=$$

(3) (8 , 10) → ☐

$$\frac{1}{8}+\frac{3}{10}=$$

(4) (8 , 12) → ☐

$$\frac{3}{8}+\frac{1}{12}=$$

(5) (9 , 12) → ☐

$$\frac{1}{9}+\frac{1}{12}=$$

(6) (6 , 15) → ☐

$$\frac{1}{6}+\frac{4}{15}=$$

2 Find the least common multiple.

2 points per question

(1) (4 , 6) → ☐   (7) (8 , 14) → ☐

(2) (9 , 12) → ☐   (8) (8 , 10) → ☐

(3) (4 , 14) → ☐   (9) (9 , 15) → ☐

(4) (4 , 11) → ☐   (10) (10 , 15) → ☐

(5) (5 , 12) → ☐   (11) (10 , 14) → ☐

(6) (10 , 12) → ☐   (12) (10 , 18) → ☐

3 Add.

4 points per question

(1) $\dfrac{3}{4}+\dfrac{1}{6}=\dfrac{\square}{12}+\dfrac{\square}{12}$

$=$

(2) $\dfrac{1}{9}+\dfrac{7}{12}=$

(3) $\dfrac{1}{4}+\dfrac{1}{14}=$

(4) $\dfrac{3}{10}+\dfrac{5}{12}=$

(5) $\dfrac{3}{8}+\dfrac{5}{14}=$

(6) $\dfrac{1}{9}+\dfrac{2}{15}=$

(7) $\dfrac{3}{10}+\dfrac{2}{15}=$

① $\dfrac{3}{10}+\dfrac{2}{15}=\dfrac{45}{150}+\dfrac{20}{150}$
$=\dfrac{65}{150}=\dfrac{13}{30}$

② $\dfrac{3}{10}+\dfrac{2}{15}=\dfrac{9}{30}+\dfrac{4}{30}$
$=\dfrac{13}{30}$

See how ① is more difficult than ② ?
Try to make sure you are working with
the LCM every time!

Wow! You're doing really well!

27

Addition of Fractions

Level ★★

Date / /

Name

Score /100

1 **Add.**

5 points per question

(1) $\dfrac{5}{6}+\dfrac{1}{10}=\dfrac{\boxed{}}{30}+\dfrac{\boxed{}}{30}$

$=\dfrac{\boxed{}}{30}=\dfrac{\boxed{}}{15}$

Remember to use the LCM when making your denominators the same!

(2) $\dfrac{1}{6}+\dfrac{2}{15}=$

(3) $\dfrac{1}{6}+\dfrac{3}{8}=$

(4) $\dfrac{1}{6}+\dfrac{5}{14}=$

(5) $\dfrac{7}{10}+\dfrac{2}{15}=$

(6) $\dfrac{1}{2}+\dfrac{2}{5}=$

(7) $\dfrac{2}{3}+\dfrac{1}{4}=$

(8) $\dfrac{1}{2}+\dfrac{3}{7}=$

(9) $\dfrac{3}{4}+\dfrac{1}{5}=$

(10) $\dfrac{1}{6}+\dfrac{3}{7}=$

2 **Add.**

(1) $\dfrac{1}{4} + \dfrac{5}{6} = \dfrac{\boxed{}}{12} + \dfrac{\boxed{}}{12}$

$\phantom{\dfrac{1}{4} + \dfrac{5}{6}} = \dfrac{\boxed{}}{12} = 1\dfrac{\boxed{}}{12}$

(2) $\dfrac{3}{4} + \dfrac{3}{10} =$

(3) $\dfrac{5}{8} + \dfrac{7}{12} =$

(4) $\dfrac{5}{6} + \dfrac{3}{8} =$

(5) $\dfrac{3}{4} + \dfrac{3}{5} =$

(6) $\dfrac{1}{2} + \dfrac{4}{7} =$

(7) $\dfrac{2}{3} + \dfrac{2}{5} =$

(8) $\dfrac{2}{3} + \dfrac{4}{7} =$

(9) $\dfrac{5}{6} + \dfrac{3}{7} =$

(10) $\dfrac{5}{8} + \dfrac{4}{9} =$

Good job! Don't forget to check your answers.

1 **Add.**

5 points per question

(1) $\dfrac{5}{6} + \dfrac{4}{15} = \dfrac{\Box}{30} + \dfrac{\Box}{30}$

$= \dfrac{\Box}{30} = \dfrac{\Box}{10} = 1\dfrac{\Box}{10}$

(2) $\dfrac{7}{10} + \dfrac{7}{15} =$

(3) $\dfrac{3}{5} + \dfrac{11}{15} =$

(4) $\dfrac{7}{8} + \dfrac{7}{24} =$

(5) $\dfrac{3}{7} + \dfrac{19}{21} =$

(6) $\dfrac{2}{3} + \dfrac{8}{15} =$

(7) $\dfrac{6}{7} + \dfrac{9}{14} =$

(8) $\dfrac{7}{10} + \dfrac{11}{20} =$

(9) $\dfrac{5}{6} + \dfrac{7}{10} =$

(10) $\dfrac{1}{5} + \dfrac{3}{10} =$

(2) **Add.**

(1) $\dfrac{1}{3} + \dfrac{5}{9} =$

(2) $\dfrac{1}{2} + \dfrac{3}{10} =$

(3) $\dfrac{3}{4} + \dfrac{3}{10} =$

(4) $\dfrac{3}{5} + \dfrac{13}{20} =$

(5) $\dfrac{5}{6} + \dfrac{5}{8} =$

(6) $\dfrac{5}{6} + \dfrac{1}{15} =$

(7) $\dfrac{9}{10} + \dfrac{4}{15} =$

(8) $\dfrac{5}{6} + \dfrac{2}{9} =$

(9) $\dfrac{5}{6} + \dfrac{9}{14} =$

(10) $\dfrac{7}{10} + \dfrac{13}{35} =$

Practice makes perfect! Let's keep going!

31

Date   /   /

Name

Score

/100

Don't forget!

There is another way to find the LCM.

Example   (8 , 12)   →   24

If you know the GCF, divide the two numbers by the GCF.

4) 8, 12 ← Divide by the GCF.
   2, 3

Then multiply the GCF by both of the resulting numbers, like this.

4×2×3= 24

When you don't know the GCF, find it first, and then follow the same procedure.

(Divide by simple common factors.)

2) 8, 12 ← Divide by 2.
2) 4, 6 ← Divide by 2.
   2, 3 ← You can't divide these any more.

2×2×2×3= 24

---

1   **Find the LCM.**

5 points per question

(1) (12, 16) → ☐

(2) (8 , 20) → ☐

(3) (12, 20) → ☐

(4) (9 , 18) → ☐

(5) (16, 20) → ☐

(6) (24, 30) → ☐

(7) (32, 48) → ☐

(8) (20, 24) → ☐

(9) (30, 48) → ☐

(10) (36, 42) → ☐

2 **Add.**

(1) $\dfrac{1}{8} + \dfrac{1}{12} = \dfrac{\square}{24} + \dfrac{\square}{24}$

$= $

(2) $\dfrac{1}{8} + \dfrac{7}{20} =$

(3) $\dfrac{5}{12} + \dfrac{3}{16} =$

(4) $\dfrac{7}{12} + \dfrac{5}{18} =$

(5) $\dfrac{5}{12} + \dfrac{7}{20} =$

(6) $\dfrac{5}{12} + \dfrac{8}{15} =$

(7) $\dfrac{8}{15} + \dfrac{3}{25} =$

(8) $\dfrac{3}{16} + \dfrac{1}{20} =$

(9) $\dfrac{7}{32} + \dfrac{5}{48} =$

(10) $\dfrac{1}{24} + \dfrac{7}{30} =$

Remember to use the LCM. Hang in there!

33

Addition of Fractions

Date   /   /

Name

Score   /100

1   **Add.**

5 points per question

(1) $\dfrac{1}{4} + \dfrac{5}{12} =$

(2) $\dfrac{1}{12} + \dfrac{5}{14} =$

(3) $\dfrac{1}{12} + \dfrac{1}{28} =$

(4) $\dfrac{2}{9} + \dfrac{7}{15} =$

(5) $\dfrac{1}{4} + \dfrac{7}{20} =$

(6) $\dfrac{1}{12} + \dfrac{3}{20} =$

(7) $\dfrac{5}{12} + \dfrac{1}{30} =$

(8) $\dfrac{1}{18} + \dfrac{1}{30} =$

(9) $\dfrac{7}{20} + \dfrac{7}{30} =$

(10) $\dfrac{11}{24} + \dfrac{11}{30} =$

2 **Add.**

(1) $\dfrac{5}{6} + \dfrac{7}{18} =$

(2) $\dfrac{5}{12} + \dfrac{11}{18} =$

(3) $\dfrac{3}{5} + \dfrac{13}{20} =$

(4) $\dfrac{5}{12} + \dfrac{13}{20} =$

(5) $\dfrac{3}{14} + \dfrac{20}{21} =$

(6) $\dfrac{7}{12} + \dfrac{9}{16} =$

(7) $\dfrac{11}{14} + \dfrac{13}{28} =$

(8) $\dfrac{7}{10} + \dfrac{12}{25} =$

(9) $\dfrac{9}{14} + \dfrac{16}{35} =$

(10) $\dfrac{13}{18} + \dfrac{11}{30} =$

If you're not sure about your answer, it never hurts to try again!

Addition of Fractions

Level ★★

Date / /

Name

Score

/100

1 **Add.**

5 points per question

(1) $1\dfrac{1}{2}+2\dfrac{1}{3}=1\dfrac{\square}{6}+2\dfrac{\square}{6}$

$\phantom{1\dfrac{1}{2}+2\dfrac{1}{3}}=3\dfrac{\square}{6}$

(2) $2\dfrac{1}{2}+1\dfrac{1}{4}=$

(3) $1\dfrac{1}{3}+1\dfrac{1}{5}=$

(4) $1\dfrac{1}{4}+2\dfrac{1}{3}=$

(5) $2\dfrac{1}{6}+1\dfrac{1}{8}=$

(6) $2\dfrac{1}{2}+\dfrac{3}{8}=$

(7) $\dfrac{2}{5}+1\dfrac{1}{3}=$

(8) $2\dfrac{3}{5}+\dfrac{2}{15}=$

(9) $1\dfrac{5}{8}+2\dfrac{3}{16}=$

(10) $2\dfrac{2}{9}+3\dfrac{3}{4}=$

2 **Add.**

(1) $1\dfrac{1}{3}+2\dfrac{3}{4}=1\dfrac{\square}{12}+2\dfrac{\square}{12}$

$\qquad =3\dfrac{\square}{12}=4\dfrac{\square}{12}$

(2) $2\dfrac{1}{3}+1\dfrac{5}{6}=$

(3) $2\dfrac{3}{4}+2\dfrac{5}{9}=$

(4) $1\dfrac{2}{3}+3\dfrac{7}{18}=$

(5) $2\dfrac{5}{6}+\dfrac{7}{12}=$

(6) $2\dfrac{1}{2}+\dfrac{2}{3}=$

(7) $\dfrac{4}{5}+1\dfrac{2}{3}=$

(8) $2\dfrac{5}{6}+\dfrac{3}{4}=$

(9) $2\dfrac{1}{8}+3\dfrac{11}{12}=$

(10) $1\dfrac{4}{9}+2\dfrac{5}{6}=$

Good job! Let's check your score!

37

1 **Add.**

5 points per question

(1) $1\dfrac{1}{6}+2\dfrac{1}{3}=1\dfrac{1}{6}+2\dfrac{\square}{6}$

$\qquad\qquad =3\dfrac{\square}{6}=$

(2) $2\dfrac{1}{4}+1\dfrac{5}{12}=$

(3) $1\dfrac{4}{9}+3\dfrac{7}{18}=$

(4) $2\dfrac{1}{6}+1\dfrac{3}{10}=$

(5) $\dfrac{3}{4}+3\dfrac{1}{20}=$

(6) $1\dfrac{7}{15}+\dfrac{5}{6}=$

(7) $\dfrac{5}{8}+1\dfrac{7}{24}=$

(8) $1\dfrac{9}{10}+2\dfrac{1}{6}=$

(9) $2\dfrac{7}{12}+3\dfrac{2}{3}=$

(10) $2\dfrac{11}{15}+1\dfrac{1}{6}=$

② **Add.**

(1) $3\frac{1}{2} + 1\frac{1}{6} =$

(2) $1\frac{1}{4} + \frac{5}{6} =$

(3) $\frac{3}{10} + 2\frac{4}{5} =$

(4) $2\frac{1}{4} + 1\frac{1}{10} =$

(5) $1\frac{3}{4} + 3\frac{5}{6} =$

(6) $1\frac{5}{6} + 2\frac{1}{12} =$

(7) $2\frac{1}{2} + \frac{9}{14} =$

(8) $1\frac{5}{6} + 1\frac{4}{15} =$

(9) $\frac{5}{7} + 2\frac{8}{21} =$

(10) $2\frac{3}{8} + 1\frac{7}{12} =$

Great! Now let's try something a little different.

20

Subtraction of Fractions

Level

Date　　/　　/

Name

Score

/100

1 **Subtract.**

5 points per question

(1) $\dfrac{1}{4} - \dfrac{1}{8} = \dfrac{\boxed{}}{8} - \dfrac{1}{8}$

$= $

(2) $\dfrac{3}{4} - \dfrac{1}{8} =$

(3) $\dfrac{3}{4} - \dfrac{3}{8} =$

(4) $\dfrac{3}{4} - \dfrac{5}{8} =$

(5) $\dfrac{1}{3} - \dfrac{1}{9} =$

(6) $\dfrac{2}{3} - \dfrac{1}{9} =$

(7) $\dfrac{2}{3} - \dfrac{2}{9} =$

(8) $\dfrac{1}{2} - \dfrac{1}{8} =$

(9) $\dfrac{1}{2} - \dfrac{3}{8} =$

(10) $\dfrac{1}{2} - \dfrac{1}{4} =$

2 **Subtract.**

(1) $\dfrac{1}{3} - \dfrac{1}{6} =$

(6) $\dfrac{4}{5} - \dfrac{1}{2} =$

(2) $\dfrac{1}{5} - \dfrac{1}{10} =$

(7) $\dfrac{1}{3} - \dfrac{1}{7} =$

(3) $\dfrac{2}{5} - \dfrac{1}{10} =$

(8) $\dfrac{1}{4} - \dfrac{1}{5} =$

(4) $\dfrac{1}{2} - \dfrac{1}{5} = \dfrac{\square}{10} - \dfrac{\square}{10}$

$=$

(9) $\dfrac{1}{3} - \dfrac{1}{5} =$

(5) $\dfrac{1}{2} - \dfrac{2}{5} =$

(10) $\dfrac{2}{5} - \dfrac{1}{3} =$

Easy, right? Let's keep going!

41

Subtraction of Fractions

Date / /

Name

Score
/100

1 **Subtract.**

5 points per question

(1) $\dfrac{2}{3} - \dfrac{1}{6} = \dfrac{\square}{6} - \dfrac{1}{6}$

$= \dfrac{\square}{6} = \dfrac{}{2}$

(2) $\dfrac{1}{2} - \dfrac{1}{6} =$

(3) $\dfrac{1}{2} - \dfrac{3}{10} =$

(4) $\dfrac{3}{5} - \dfrac{1}{10} =$

(5) $\dfrac{4}{5} - \dfrac{3}{10} =$

(6) $\dfrac{1}{4} - \dfrac{1}{12} =$

(7) $\dfrac{3}{4} - \dfrac{5}{12} =$

(8) $\dfrac{5}{6} - \dfrac{7}{12} =$

(9) $\dfrac{8}{15} - \dfrac{1}{5} =$

(10) $\dfrac{7}{18} - \dfrac{1}{6} =$

2 **Subtract.**

(1) $\dfrac{3}{4} - \dfrac{1}{6} = \dfrac{\square}{12} - \dfrac{\square}{12}$

$=$

(6) $\dfrac{5}{8} - \dfrac{5}{12} =$

(2) $\dfrac{1}{6} - \dfrac{1}{8} =$

(7) $\dfrac{9}{10} - \dfrac{1}{15} =$

(3) $\dfrac{5}{6} - \dfrac{2}{9} =$

(8) $\dfrac{7}{10} - \dfrac{1}{6} =$

(4) $\dfrac{5}{6} - \dfrac{1}{10} =$

(9) $\dfrac{5}{14} - \dfrac{3}{10} =$

(5) $\dfrac{5}{6} - \dfrac{3}{10} =$

(10) $\dfrac{7}{18} - \dfrac{3}{10} =$

Excellent. Don't forget to keep using the LCM!

22

Subtraction of Fractions

Level

Date / /

Name

Score

/100

1 **Subtract.**

(1) $\dfrac{5}{4} - \dfrac{3}{8} = \dfrac{\boxed{}}{8} - \dfrac{3}{8}$

$=$

(2) $\dfrac{5}{4} - \dfrac{5}{8} =$

(3) $\dfrac{3}{2} - \dfrac{5}{8} =$

(4) $\dfrac{9}{8} - \dfrac{1}{4} =$

(5) $\dfrac{7}{6} - \dfrac{1}{3} =$

(6) $\dfrac{4}{3} - \dfrac{2}{5} = \dfrac{\boxed{}}{15} - \dfrac{\boxed{}}{15}$

$=$

(7) $\dfrac{7}{5} - \dfrac{1}{2} =$

(8) $\dfrac{7}{4} - \dfrac{5}{6} =$

(9) $\dfrac{7}{6} - \dfrac{5}{8} =$

(10) $\dfrac{10}{9} - \dfrac{5}{6} =$

2 **Subtract.**

(1) $\dfrac{4}{3} - \dfrac{5}{6} = \dfrac{\square}{6} - \dfrac{5}{6}$

$\phantom{\dfrac{4}{3} - \dfrac{5}{6}} = \dfrac{\square}{6} =$

(2) $\dfrac{3}{2} - \dfrac{7}{10} =$

(3) $\dfrac{7}{5} - \dfrac{9}{10} =$

(4) $\dfrac{4}{3} - \dfrac{7}{12} =$

(5) $\dfrac{5}{4} - \dfrac{5}{12} =$

(6) $\dfrac{16}{15} - \dfrac{2}{3} =$

(7) $\dfrac{7}{6} - \dfrac{3}{10} =$

(8) $\dfrac{17}{15} - \dfrac{5}{6} =$

(9) $\dfrac{11}{10} - \dfrac{4}{15} =$

(10) $\dfrac{15}{14} - \dfrac{5}{21} =$

You're doing great. Did you solve your problems without mistakes?

45

1 **Subtract.**

5 points per question

(1) $2\dfrac{1}{2} - 1\dfrac{1}{3} = 2\dfrac{\square}{6} - 1\dfrac{\square}{6}$

$\quad\quad\quad = 1\dfrac{\square}{6}$

(2) $3\dfrac{1}{3} - 2\dfrac{1}{4} = 3\dfrac{\square}{12} - 2\dfrac{\square}{12}$

$\quad\quad\quad =$

(3) $2\dfrac{3}{5} - \dfrac{3}{10} =$

(4) $3\dfrac{7}{9} - \dfrac{1}{3} =$

(5) $4\dfrac{5}{12} - 1\dfrac{3}{8} =$

(6) $2\dfrac{3}{4} - 1\dfrac{1}{2} =$

(7) $3\dfrac{6}{7} - 1\dfrac{2}{3} =$

(8) $2\dfrac{7}{9} - \dfrac{5}{12} =$

(9) $3\dfrac{5}{6} - 2\dfrac{3}{4} =$

(10) $2\dfrac{7}{8} - 1\dfrac{2}{3} =$

2 **Subtract.**

(1) $3\dfrac{1}{4} - 1\dfrac{2}{3} = 3\dfrac{\square}{12} - 1\dfrac{\square}{12}$

$\qquad = 2\dfrac{\boxed{}}{12} - 1\dfrac{\square}{12}$

$\qquad =$

(2) $4\dfrac{1}{6} - 2\dfrac{8}{9} = 4\dfrac{\square}{18} - 2\dfrac{\boxed{}}{18}$

$\qquad =$

(3) $4\dfrac{1}{3} - 1\dfrac{2}{5} =$

(4) $2\dfrac{1}{4} - \dfrac{1}{2} =$

(5) $3\dfrac{1}{7} - \dfrac{1}{3} =$

(6) $1\dfrac{1}{5} - \dfrac{5}{6} =$

(7) $2\dfrac{2}{3} - \dfrac{7}{9} =$

(8) $2\dfrac{3}{10} - 1\dfrac{3}{4} =$

(9) $3\dfrac{5}{8} - 2\dfrac{5}{6} =$

(10) $4\dfrac{2}{7} - 1\dfrac{5}{14} =$

If a problem looks tricky, just think about it a bit more.

47

Subtraction of Fractions

Date / /

Name

Score

/100

1 **Subtract.**

5 points per question

(1) $2\dfrac{2}{3} - 1\dfrac{1}{6} = 2\dfrac{\square}{6} - 1\dfrac{1}{6}$

$\qquad = 1\dfrac{\square}{6} =$

(2) $3\dfrac{7}{12} - 1\dfrac{1}{3} =$

(3) $1\dfrac{1}{6} - \dfrac{1}{10} =$

(4) $2\dfrac{2}{3} - \dfrac{5}{12} =$

(5) $3\dfrac{5}{7} - 2\dfrac{3}{14} =$

(6) $3\dfrac{3}{10} - 1\dfrac{4}{5} = 3\dfrac{3}{10} - 1\dfrac{\square}{10}$

$\qquad = 2\dfrac{\square}{10} - 1\dfrac{\square}{10}$

$\qquad = 1\dfrac{\square}{10} =$

(7) $4\dfrac{1}{6} - 2\dfrac{2}{3} =$

(8) $3\dfrac{1}{10} - 1\dfrac{5}{6} =$

(9) $2\dfrac{1}{4} - \dfrac{5}{12} =$

(10) $1\dfrac{11}{15} - \dfrac{9}{10} =$

2 Subtract.

(1) $\dfrac{5}{6} - \dfrac{2}{3} =$

(2) $\dfrac{3}{4} - \dfrac{1}{6} =$

(3) $\dfrac{5}{3} - \dfrac{3}{4} =$

(4) $2\dfrac{1}{4} - \dfrac{1}{2} =$

(5) $3\dfrac{3}{7} - 1\dfrac{5}{14} =$

(6) $\dfrac{1}{6} - \dfrac{1}{10} =$

(7) $3\dfrac{5}{6} - 2\dfrac{1}{2} =$

(8) $2\dfrac{1}{3} - \dfrac{7}{9} =$

(9) $3\dfrac{1}{2} - \dfrac{7}{10} =$

(10) $4\dfrac{1}{2} - 3\dfrac{5}{6} =$

Remember, practice makes perfect!

Three Fractions

Date / /

Name

Level ★★★

Score /100

1 **Add.**

4 points per question

(1) $\dfrac{1}{2} + \dfrac{1}{3} + \dfrac{1}{7} = \dfrac{\boxed{}}{42} + \dfrac{\boxed{}}{42} + \dfrac{\boxed{}}{42}$

$=$

(6) $\dfrac{1}{2} + \dfrac{1}{3} + \dfrac{1}{5} =$

(2) $\dfrac{1}{2} + \dfrac{1}{5} + \dfrac{1}{7} =$

(7) $\dfrac{1}{2} + \dfrac{2}{3} + \dfrac{4}{5} =$

(3) $\dfrac{1}{2} + \dfrac{1}{5} + \dfrac{1}{9} =$

(8) $\dfrac{1}{3} + \dfrac{1}{5} + \dfrac{1}{4} =$

(4) $\dfrac{1}{2} + \dfrac{1}{5} + \dfrac{4}{9} = \dfrac{\boxed{}}{90} + \dfrac{\boxed{}}{90} + \dfrac{\boxed{}}{90}$

$= \dfrac{\boxed{}}{90} = 1\dfrac{\boxed{}}{90}$

(9) $\dfrac{1}{3} + \dfrac{2}{5} + \dfrac{3}{4} =$

(5) $\dfrac{1}{2} + \dfrac{2}{5} + \dfrac{3}{7} =$

(10) $\dfrac{2}{3} + \dfrac{4}{5} + \dfrac{3}{4} =$

2 Find the LCM of (4, 6, 9) using the way below. (Find the LCM of the first pair of numbers first. Then find the LCM of that number and the third number.)

6 points per question

(1) The LCM of 4 and 6 is ( ).

The LCM of ( ) and 9 is ☐.

(2) The LCM of 6 and 9 is ( ).

The LCM of ( ) and 4 is ☐.

(3) The LCM of 4 and 9 is ( ).

The LCM of ( ) and 6 is ☐.

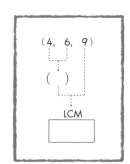

(4, 6, 9)

( )

LCM

3 Find the LCM of each group of numbers.

3 points per question

(1) (2, 3, 4) → ☐   (6) (2, 6, 8) → ☐   (11) (4, 6, 18) → ☐

(2) (2, 3, 9) → ☐   (7) (3, 4, 10) → ☐   (12) (4, 7, 14) → ☐

(3) (2, 4, 6) → ☐   (8) (3, 5, 6) → ☐   (13) (5, 6, 9) → ☐

(4) (2, 4, 14) → ☐   (9) (3, 6, 8) → ☐   (14) (6, 8, 12) → ☐

(5) (2, 5, 12) → ☐   (10) (4, 5, 6) → ☐

Here is a way to find the LCM of three numbers.

Example (4, 6, 9) → ☐ 36   **Example** (6, 8, 16) → ☐ 48

2) 4, 6, 9   ← Keep dividing the divisible →   2) 6, 8, 16
3) 2, 3, 9   numbers in the group by   2) 3, 4, 8
   2, 1, 3   two and three. Just write   2) 3, 2, 4
                 an indivisible number down   3, 1, 2
                 again. Then multiply all the
                 results together to get the
                 LCM.

                                                  $2 \times 2 \times 2 \times 3 \times 1 \times 2 =$ ☐ 48

$2 \times 3 \times 2 \times 1 \times 3 =$ ☐ 36

Great! Now let's check your answers.

26 Three Fractions

Date   /   /

Name

Level ★★★

Score

/100

---

1 Add.

5 points per question

(1) $\dfrac{1}{2} + \dfrac{1}{3} + \dfrac{1}{4} = \dfrac{\square}{12} + \dfrac{\square}{12} + \dfrac{\square}{12}$

$= \dfrac{\square}{12} = 1\dfrac{\square}{12}$

(2) $\dfrac{1}{2} + \dfrac{1}{3} + \dfrac{1}{8} =$

(3) $\dfrac{1}{2} + \dfrac{1}{4} + \dfrac{1}{10} =$

(4) $\dfrac{1}{2} + \dfrac{1}{5} + \dfrac{1}{8} =$

(5) $\dfrac{1}{3} + \dfrac{1}{4} + \dfrac{1}{8} =$

(6) $\dfrac{1}{2} + \dfrac{1}{3} + \dfrac{5}{6} =$

(7) $\dfrac{1}{2} + \dfrac{3}{4} + \dfrac{1}{6} =$

(8) $\dfrac{1}{3} + \dfrac{1}{4} + \dfrac{5}{6} =$

(9) $\dfrac{1}{4} + \dfrac{5}{6} + \dfrac{4}{9} =$

(10) $\dfrac{1}{6} + \dfrac{5}{8} + \dfrac{7}{12} =$

② Calculate.

(1) $\dfrac{1}{2} + \dfrac{1}{3} - \dfrac{1}{4} = \dfrac{\square}{12} + \dfrac{\square}{12} - \dfrac{\square}{12}$

$\qquad\qquad = \dfrac{\square}{12}$

(2) $\dfrac{1}{3} + \dfrac{1}{4} - \dfrac{1}{5} =$

(3) $\dfrac{1}{3} + \dfrac{3}{4} - \dfrac{5}{6} = \dfrac{\square}{12} + \dfrac{\square}{12} - \dfrac{\square}{12}$

$\qquad\qquad = \dfrac{\square}{12} =$

(4) $\dfrac{2}{3} + \dfrac{2}{5} - \dfrac{5}{6} =$

(5) $\dfrac{7}{8} - \dfrac{1}{2} - \dfrac{1}{3} =$

(6) $\dfrac{3}{4} - \dfrac{1}{6} - \dfrac{3}{8} =$

(7) $\dfrac{11}{8} - \dfrac{5}{6} - \dfrac{1}{3} =$

(8) $\dfrac{5}{6} - \dfrac{1}{2} + \dfrac{3}{8} =$

(9) $\dfrac{3}{8} - \dfrac{2}{9} + \dfrac{2}{3} =$

(10) $\dfrac{3}{4} - \dfrac{4}{9} + \dfrac{1}{6} =$

Don't forget to use the LCM to make all the denominators the same before you do your calculations!

Multiplication of Fractions

Date / /

Name

Score

/100

1 **Multiply.**

5 points per question

Example $\dfrac{2}{3} \times \dfrac{4}{5} = \dfrac{2 \times 4}{3 \times 5} = \dfrac{8}{15}$

(1) $\dfrac{2}{3} \times \dfrac{4}{7} = \dfrac{2 \times 4}{3 \times 7} = \dfrac{\square}{21}$

(6) $\dfrac{2}{3} \times \dfrac{1}{5} =$

(2) $\dfrac{3}{5} \times \dfrac{1}{2} =$

(7) $\dfrac{1}{5} \times \dfrac{3}{4} =$

(3) $\dfrac{1}{4} \times \dfrac{3}{5} =$

(8) $\dfrac{3}{4} \times \dfrac{3}{7} =$

(4) $\dfrac{1}{4} \times \dfrac{5}{6} =$

(9) $\dfrac{3}{7} \times \dfrac{2}{5} =$

(5) $\dfrac{1}{3} \times \dfrac{5}{7} =$

(10) $\dfrac{3}{5} \times \dfrac{3}{8} =$

2 Multiply.

(1) $\dfrac{2}{5} \times \dfrac{3}{7} =$

(2) $\dfrac{4}{7} \times \dfrac{3}{5} =$

(3) $\dfrac{3}{7} \times \dfrac{3}{8} =$

(4) $\dfrac{1}{6} \times \dfrac{5}{7} =$

(5) $\dfrac{5}{6} \times \dfrac{1}{8} =$

(6) $\dfrac{5}{6} \times \dfrac{5}{7} =$

(7) $\dfrac{5}{6} \times \dfrac{7}{9} =$

(8) $\dfrac{2}{7} \times \dfrac{4}{9} =$

(9) $\dfrac{3}{8} \times \dfrac{5}{7} =$

(10) $\dfrac{7}{8} \times \dfrac{5}{9} =$

Show your parents how far you've come!

55

Level ★ ★

Date   /   /

Name

Score
/100

1 **Multiply and reduce along the way.**

5 points per question

Example $\dfrac{6}{7} \times \dfrac{5}{9} = \dfrac{\overset{2}{\cancel{6}} \times 5}{7 \times \underset{3}{\cancel{9}}} = \dfrac{10}{21}$

Reducing as you go along will make the problem easier!

(1) $\dfrac{3}{4} \times \dfrac{5}{6} = \dfrac{\overset{1}{\cancel{3}} \times 5}{4 \times \underset{2}{\cancel{6}}} = \dfrac{\square}{8}$

(6) $\dfrac{3}{4} \times \dfrac{4}{5} =$

(2) $\dfrac{2}{3} \times \dfrac{1}{4} =$

(7) $\dfrac{4}{5} \times \dfrac{5}{7} =$

(3) $\dfrac{2}{5} \times \dfrac{3}{4} =$

(8) $\dfrac{2}{3} \times \dfrac{6}{7} =$

(4) $\dfrac{3}{5} \times \dfrac{1}{6} =$

(9) $\dfrac{5}{6} \times \dfrac{4}{7} =$

(5) $\dfrac{4}{5} \times \dfrac{1}{2} =$

(10) $\dfrac{1}{4} \times \dfrac{6}{7} =$

2 **Multiply and reduce along the way.**

(1) $\dfrac{3}{8} \times \dfrac{2}{5} =$

(2) $\dfrac{4}{5} \times \dfrac{3}{8} =$

(3) $\dfrac{5}{8} \times \dfrac{2}{3} =$

(4) $\dfrac{6}{7} \times \dfrac{5}{8} =$

(5) $\dfrac{7}{8} \times \dfrac{5}{7} =$

(6) $\dfrac{5}{9} \times \dfrac{4}{5} =$

(7) $\dfrac{9}{10} \times \dfrac{1}{6} =$

(8) $\dfrac{6}{7} \times \dfrac{3}{10} =$

(9) $\dfrac{7}{12} \times \dfrac{8}{9} =$

(10) $\dfrac{4}{11} \times \dfrac{5}{6} =$

If you're not sure about your answer, just try the problem again!

Multiplication of Fractions

Level ★★

1 **Multiply and reduce along the way.**

5 points per question

Example

$$\frac{3}{4} \times \frac{8}{9} = \frac{\overset{1}{\cancel{3}} \times \overset{2}{\cancel{8}}}{\underset{1}{\cancel{4}} \times \underset{3}{\cancel{9}}}$$

$$= \frac{2}{3}$$

(1) $\dfrac{2}{3} \times \dfrac{3}{4} = \dfrac{\overset{\square}{\cancel{2}}}{\underset{1}{\cancel{3}}} \times \dfrac{\overset{1}{\cancel{3}}}{\underset{\square}{\cancel{4}}}$

$=$

(2) $\dfrac{4}{5} \times \dfrac{5}{12} =$

(3) $\dfrac{5}{6} \times \dfrac{9}{10} =$

(4) $\dfrac{3}{10} \times \dfrac{5}{6} =$

(5) $\dfrac{3}{4} \times \dfrac{8}{9} =$

(6) $\dfrac{7}{9} \times \dfrac{3}{7} =$

(7) $\dfrac{3}{14} \times \dfrac{7}{9} =$

(8) $\dfrac{3}{10} \times \dfrac{5}{12} =$

2 **Multiply and reduce along the way.**

6 points per question

(1) $\dfrac{3}{5} \times \dfrac{5}{6} =$

(2) $\dfrac{4}{7} \times \dfrac{7}{8} =$

(3) $\dfrac{3}{4} \times \dfrac{8}{15} =$

(4) $\dfrac{7}{10} \times \dfrac{5}{14} =$

(5) $\dfrac{5}{6} \times \dfrac{18}{25} =$

(6) $\dfrac{5}{8} \times \dfrac{2}{15} =$

(7) $\dfrac{8}{15} \times \dfrac{5}{12} =$

(8) $\dfrac{7}{12} \times \dfrac{9}{14} =$

(9) $\dfrac{7}{18} \times \dfrac{15}{28} =$

(10) $\dfrac{9}{16} \times \dfrac{20}{27} =$

Don't forget to check your answers when you're done.

59

Multiplication of Fractions

Score

/100

Date / /

Name

1 Multiply.

5 points per question

Example

$$\frac{2}{5} \times 3 = \frac{2}{5} \times \frac{3}{1}$$

$$= \frac{2 \times 3}{5} = \frac{6}{5} = 1\frac{1}{5}$$

When multiplying a fraction with an integer, first change the integer into the form of a fraction like this: $\frac{\square}{1}$.

(1) $\dfrac{4}{5} \times 2 = \dfrac{4}{5} \times \dfrac{\boxed{2}}{1}$

$=$

(2) $\dfrac{3}{7} \times 2 =$

(3) $\dfrac{3}{8} \times 3 =$

(4) $\dfrac{4}{9} \times 2 =$

(5) $\dfrac{4}{11} \times 3 =$

(6) $3 \times \dfrac{3}{5} =$

(7) $4 \times \dfrac{2}{7} =$

(8) $5 \times \dfrac{2}{13} =$

(9) $4 \times \dfrac{3}{17} =$

(10) $6 \times \dfrac{2}{11} =$

2 **Multiply and reduce along the way.**

5 points per question

(1) $2 \times \dfrac{1}{5} =$

(2) $\dfrac{5}{12} \times 2 = \dfrac{5}{\cancel{12}_{6}} \times \dfrac{\cancel{2}^{1}}{1}$

$=$

(3) $\dfrac{3}{14} \times 2 =$

(4) $3 \times \dfrac{4}{15} =$

(5) $4 \times \dfrac{5}{12} =$

(6) $\dfrac{5}{8} \times 2 =$

(7) $\dfrac{7}{8} \times 6 =$

(8) $8 \times \dfrac{5}{12} =$

(9) $9 \times \dfrac{7}{15} =$

(10) $\dfrac{2}{21} \times 6 =$

You're doing really well!

31 Multiplication of Fractions

Level ★★

Date   /   /

Name

Score

/100

1 Multiply.

6 points per question

Example

$$1\frac{1}{2} \times 1\frac{3}{4} = \frac{3}{2} \times \frac{7}{4}$$

$$= \frac{21}{8} = 2\frac{5}{8}$$

Before multiplying, change any mixed numbers to improper fractions.

(1) $1\frac{2}{5} \times \frac{3}{4} = \frac{\square}{5} \times \frac{3}{4}$

$=$

(2) $2\frac{1}{3} \times \frac{2}{5} =$

(3) $\frac{3}{4} \times 2\frac{1}{7} = \frac{3}{4} \times \frac{\boxed{}}{7}$

$=$

(4) $2\frac{1}{2} \times 2\frac{1}{3} =$

(5) $2\frac{3}{5} \times 1\frac{1}{6} =$

(6) $1\frac{3}{8} \times 1\frac{2}{3} =$

(7) $1\frac{3}{5} \times 2\frac{1}{9} =$

(8) $2\frac{1}{6} \times \frac{5}{7} =$

(9) $1\frac{3}{4} \times 3 =$

(10) $4 \times 2\frac{2}{7} =$

② Multiply and reduce along the way.

Example
$$2\frac{2}{3} \times 1\frac{1}{6} = \frac{8}{3} \times \frac{7}{6}$$
$$= \frac{\overset{4}{\cancel{8}} \times 7}{3 \times \cancel{6}_{3}} = \frac{28}{9} = 3\frac{1}{9}$$

(1) $2\frac{1}{3} \times \frac{3}{4} = \frac{7}{\cancel{3}_{1}} \times \frac{\cancel{3}^{1}}{4}$

$= \frac{\square}{4} =$

(2) $1\frac{1}{2} \times \frac{4}{5} =$

(3) $\frac{3}{4} \times 2\frac{2}{5} =$

(4) $3\frac{1}{2} \times 2\frac{1}{7} =$

(5) $2\frac{2}{7} \times 1\frac{3}{8} =$

(6) $1\frac{2}{9} \times \frac{3}{5} =$

(7) $1\frac{5}{6} \times 3 =$

(8) $1\frac{3}{4} \times 6 =$

Excellent! Remember to write your answers as mixed numbers when appropriate!

Multiplication of Fractions

Date / /

Name

Score
/100

1 **Multiply and reduce along the way.**

5 points per question

Example
$$1\frac{1}{3} \times 1\frac{1}{8} = \frac{4}{3} \times \frac{9}{8}$$
$$= \frac{\overset{1}{\cancel{4}} \times \overset{3}{\cancel{9}}}{\underset{1}{\cancel{3}} \times \underset{2}{\cancel{8}}} = \frac{3}{2} = 1\frac{1}{2}$$

(1) $2\frac{1}{4} \times \frac{2}{3} = \frac{\overset{3}{\cancel{9}}}{\underset{2}{\cancel{4}}} \times \frac{\overset{1}{\cancel{2}}}{\underset{1}{\cancel{3}}}$

$$= \frac{\square}{2} =$$

(5) $1\frac{1}{2} \times 1\frac{1}{3} =$

(2) $3\frac{3}{4} \times \frac{2}{3} =$

(6) $1\frac{2}{3} \times 1\frac{1}{5} =$

(3) $\frac{3}{5} \times 1\frac{2}{3} =$

(7) $2\frac{2}{5} \times 1\frac{7}{8} =$

(4) $\frac{3}{5} \times 3\frac{1}{3} =$

(8) $2\frac{1}{7} \times 3\frac{1}{9} =$

2 Multiply.

(1) $\dfrac{2}{3} \times \dfrac{4}{5} =$

(6) $\dfrac{5}{6} \times 4 =$

(2) $\dfrac{6}{7} \times \dfrac{7}{9} =$

(7) $\dfrac{7}{15} \times \dfrac{9}{14} =$

(3) $\dfrac{3}{4} \times \dfrac{8}{9} =$

(8) $1\dfrac{1}{7} \times \dfrac{5}{8} =$

(4) $1\dfrac{5}{6} \times \dfrac{5}{9} =$

(9) $1\dfrac{2}{5} \times 3\dfrac{4}{7} =$

(5) $1\dfrac{3}{5} \times 2\dfrac{1}{7} =$

(10) $2\dfrac{8}{9} \times 1\dfrac{7}{8} =$

Well done. Now it's time for another step forward!

65

33 Division of Fractions

Level ★★

Date / /

Name

Score

/100

1 Divide.

5 points per question

Example
$$\frac{3}{7} \div \frac{5}{6} = \frac{3}{7} \times \frac{6}{5}$$
$$= \frac{18}{35}$$

When dividing fractions, invert the second fraction so that the denominator is on top, and then multiply!

(1) $\dfrac{4}{5} \div \dfrac{3}{7} = \dfrac{4}{5} \times \dfrac{\boxed{}}{\boxed{}}$

$=$

(2) $\dfrac{3}{7} \div \dfrac{4}{5} =$

(3) $\dfrac{2}{5} \div \dfrac{7}{9} =$

(4) $\dfrac{7}{9} \div \dfrac{2}{5} =$

(5) $\dfrac{5}{6} \div \dfrac{3}{7} =$

(6) $\dfrac{5}{8} \div \dfrac{2}{7} =$

(7) $\dfrac{2}{7} \div \dfrac{5}{8} =$

(8) $\dfrac{5}{9} \div \dfrac{4}{7} =$

(9) $\dfrac{4}{7} \div \dfrac{5}{9} =$

(10) $\dfrac{3}{7} \div \dfrac{5}{6} =$

2 **Divide.**

(1) $\dfrac{2}{5} \div \dfrac{3}{7} =$

(2) $\dfrac{3}{4} \div \dfrac{2}{5} =$

(3) $\dfrac{2}{7} \div \dfrac{5}{9} =$

(4) $\dfrac{1}{4} \div \dfrac{2}{3} =$

(5) $\dfrac{2}{3} \div \dfrac{1}{5} =$

(6) $\dfrac{3}{7} \div \dfrac{2}{5} =$

(7) $\dfrac{4}{5} \div \dfrac{7}{9} =$

(8) $\dfrac{8}{9} \div \dfrac{7}{10} =$

(9) $\dfrac{5}{8} \div \dfrac{4}{9} =$

(10) $\dfrac{7}{12} \div \dfrac{4}{5} =$

Not so bad, right? Good job!

34 Division of Fractions

Level ★★

Date   /   /

Name

Score
/100

1 Divide and reduce along the way.

5 points per question

Example

$$\frac{5}{6} \div \frac{3}{4} = \frac{5}{\overset{3}{\cancel{6}}} \times \frac{\overset{2}{\cancel{4}}}{3}$$

$$= \frac{10}{9} = 1\frac{1}{9}$$

Reducing as you go along will make the problem easier!

(1) $\dfrac{4}{5} \div \dfrac{2}{3} = \dfrac{4}{5} \times \dfrac{3}{\underset{1}{\cancel{2}}}$

$=$

(2) $\dfrac{3}{4} \div \dfrac{3}{7} =$

(3) $\dfrac{7}{8} \div \dfrac{5}{8} =$

(4) $\dfrac{2}{3} \div \dfrac{2}{7} =$

(5) $\dfrac{2}{5} \div \dfrac{4}{7} =$

(6) $\dfrac{5}{6} \div \dfrac{2}{3} =$

(7) $\dfrac{6}{7} \div \dfrac{4}{5} =$

(8) $\dfrac{1}{4} \div \dfrac{3}{8} =$

(9) $\dfrac{1}{4} \div \dfrac{27}{28} =$

(10) $\dfrac{1}{2} \div \dfrac{13}{18} =$

2 **Divide and reduce along the way.**

(1) $\dfrac{3}{4} \div \dfrac{5}{8} =$

(6) $\dfrac{7}{8} \div \dfrac{5}{6} =$

(2) $\dfrac{5}{9} \div \dfrac{2}{3} =$

(7) $\dfrac{1}{6} \div \dfrac{4}{9} =$

(3) $\dfrac{6}{7} \div \dfrac{4}{5} =$

(8) $\dfrac{2}{5} \div \dfrac{7}{15} =$

(4) $\dfrac{1}{3} \div \dfrac{5}{6} =$

(9) $\dfrac{8}{9} \div \dfrac{10}{11} =$

(5) $\dfrac{7}{8} \div \dfrac{1}{4} =$

(10) $\dfrac{3}{10} \div \dfrac{14}{25} =$

Nicely done! Let's keep going!

69

Date / /

Name

1 Divide.

5 points per question

Example
$$\frac{5}{7} \div 2 = \frac{5}{7} \div \frac{2}{1}$$
$$= \frac{5}{7} \times \frac{1}{2} = \frac{5}{14}$$

When dividing a fraction by an integer, first change the integer into the form of a fraction like this: $\frac{\square}{1}$. Then invert that fraction.

(1) $\frac{1}{7} \div 2 =$

(2) $\frac{1}{2} \div 6 =$

(3) $\frac{2}{3} \div 3 =$

(4) $\frac{6}{7} \div 5 =$

(5) $\frac{3}{10} \div 5 =$

(6) $3 \div \frac{1}{4} = \frac{3}{1} \times \frac{4}{1}$
$$=$$

(7) $1 \div \frac{1}{2} =$

(8) $4 \div \frac{3}{5} =$

(9) $5 \div \frac{4}{7} =$

(10) $4 \div \frac{5}{8} =$

2 Divide and reduce along the way.

5 points per question

Example $\dfrac{6}{7} \div 4 = \dfrac{\overset{3}{\cancel{6}}}{7} \times \dfrac{1}{\underset{2}{\cancel{4}}}$

$= \dfrac{3}{14}$

(1) $\dfrac{4}{7} \div 2 =$

(2) $\dfrac{6}{7} \div 3 =$

(3) $\dfrac{4}{5} \div 6 =$

(4) $\dfrac{9}{10} \div 6 =$

(5) $\dfrac{9}{20} \div 12 =$

(6) $3 \div \dfrac{3}{4} =$

(7) $5 \div \dfrac{5}{9} =$

(8) $6 \div \dfrac{4}{7} =$

(9) $4 \div \dfrac{2}{9} =$

(10) $8 \div \dfrac{10}{11} =$

Just take it step by step. You're doing very well!

1 **Divide and reduce along the way.**

5 points per question

Example

$$\frac{8}{9} \div \frac{4}{15} = \frac{\overset{2}{\cancel{8}}}{\underset{3}{\cancel{9}}} \times \frac{\overset{5}{\cancel{15}}}{\underset{1}{\cancel{4}}}$$

$$= \frac{10}{3} = 3\frac{1}{3}$$

(1) $\dfrac{8}{21} \div \dfrac{4}{7} = \dfrac{\overset{2}{\cancel{8}}}{\underset{\square}{\cancel{21}}} \times \dfrac{\overset{\square}{\cancel{7}}}{\underset{1}{\cancel{4}}}$

$=$

(2) $\dfrac{8}{21} \div \dfrac{2}{7} =$

(3) $\dfrac{5}{12} \div \dfrac{5}{8} =$

(4) $\dfrac{4}{5} \div \dfrac{8}{15} =$

(5) $\dfrac{9}{10} \div \dfrac{3}{4} =$

(6) $\dfrac{3}{5} \div \dfrac{9}{10} =$

(7) $\dfrac{7}{12} \div \dfrac{14}{15} =$

(8) $\dfrac{20}{27} \div \dfrac{8}{9} =$

72 © Kumon Publishing Co., Ltd.

2 Divide and reduce along the way.

6 points per question

(1) $\dfrac{9}{4} \div \dfrac{3}{8} = \dfrac{\cancel{9}}{\cancel{4}} \times \dfrac{\cancel{8}^2}{\cancel{3}} = \dfrac{\square}{1} \quad \square$

$= $

(2) $\dfrac{5}{3} \div \dfrac{5}{6} =$

(3) $\dfrac{10}{7} \div \dfrac{5}{14} =$

(4) $\dfrac{12}{7} \div \dfrac{9}{14} =$

(5) $\dfrac{15}{12} \div \dfrac{5}{9} =$

(6) $\dfrac{3}{4} \div \dfrac{9}{8} =$

(7) $\dfrac{5}{6} \div \dfrac{10}{9} =$

(8) $\dfrac{4}{9} \div \dfrac{16}{15} =$

(9) $\dfrac{8}{15} \div \dfrac{12}{5} =$

(10) $\dfrac{7}{16} \div \dfrac{21}{20} =$

Outstanding! Did you remember to check your answers?

73

Division of Fractions

Date / /

Name

Score
/ 100

1 Divide.

6 points per question

Example $1\frac{2}{7} \div 1\frac{1}{3} = \frac{9}{7} \div \frac{4}{3}$

$= \frac{9}{7} \times \frac{3}{4} = \frac{27}{28}$

Before dividing, change any mixed numbers to improper fractions.

(1) $1\frac{3}{4} \div \frac{2}{3} = \frac{7}{4} \div \frac{2}{3}$

$=$

(2) $1\frac{1}{2} \div \frac{5}{7} =$

(3) $1\frac{2}{7} \div \frac{4}{5} =$

(4) $1\frac{5}{8} \div 2\frac{1}{3} =$

(5) $\frac{3}{4} \div 1\frac{2}{3} =$

(6) $2\frac{3}{5} \div 1\frac{3}{4} =$

(7) $3\frac{2}{3} \div 1\frac{1}{4} =$

(8) $2\frac{1}{3} \div \frac{3}{7} =$

(9) $2\frac{1}{2} \div 3 =$

(10) $5 \div 1\frac{2}{7} =$

2 Divide and reduce along the way.

Example

$$2\frac{1}{3} \div 1\frac{1}{3} = \frac{7}{3} \div \frac{4}{3}$$

$$= \frac{7}{\overset{1}{\cancel{3}}} \times \frac{\overset{1}{\cancel{3}}}{4} = \frac{7}{4} = 1\frac{3}{4}$$

(1) $2\frac{1}{3} \div \frac{4}{9} = \frac{7}{3} \div \frac{4}{9}$

$$= \frac{7}{\cancel{3}} \times \frac{\overset{3}{\cancel{9}}}{4}$$

$$=$$

(2) $2\frac{2}{7} \div \frac{8}{9} =$

(3) $1\frac{4}{5} \div \frac{6}{7} =$

(4) $1\frac{1}{5} \div 1\frac{1}{2} =$

(5) $\frac{2}{3} \div 1\frac{1}{6} =$

(6) $\frac{4}{5} \div 1\frac{3}{10} =$

(7) $1\frac{3}{7} \div 1\frac{1}{4} =$

(8) $2\frac{2}{5} \div 1\frac{1}{8} =$

Remember to make the mixed numbers into improper fractions first!

Division of Fractions

Date / /

Name

Score /100

---

1 **Divide and reduce along the way.**

5 points per question

Example

$$1\frac{5}{9} \div 1\frac{1}{6} = \frac{14}{9} \div \frac{7}{6}$$

$$= \frac{\overset{2}{\cancel{14}}}{\underset{3}{\cancel{9}}} \times \frac{\overset{2}{\cancel{6}}}{\underset{1}{\cancel{7}}} = \frac{4}{3} = 1\frac{1}{3}$$

(1) $\quad 1\frac{1}{8} \div \frac{3}{4} =$

(5) $\quad \frac{5}{9} \div 1\frac{2}{3} =$

(2) $\quad 2\frac{2}{9} \div \frac{5}{6} =$

(6) $\quad \frac{5}{8} \div 3\frac{3}{4} =$

(3) $\quad 1\frac{2}{7} \div \frac{9}{14} =$

(7) $\quad 2\frac{1}{4} \div 1\frac{1}{8} =$

(4) $\quad 2\frac{2}{3} \div 1\frac{1}{9} =$

(8) $\quad 1\frac{5}{9} \div 2\frac{1}{3} =$

2 **Divide.**

(1) $\dfrac{4}{7} \div \dfrac{3}{5} =$

(6) $8 \div \dfrac{6}{7} =$

(2) $\dfrac{5}{6} \div \dfrac{3}{8} =$

(7) $6 \div 2\dfrac{1}{4} =$

(3) $\dfrac{4}{9} \div \dfrac{8}{15} =$

(8) $2\dfrac{1}{3} \div \dfrac{14}{15} =$

(4) $\dfrac{5}{6} \div 1\dfrac{3}{4} =$

(9) $1\dfrac{5}{6} \div 2\dfrac{1}{3} =$

(5) $2\dfrac{4}{5} \div 2\dfrac{2}{3} =$

(10) $2\dfrac{1}{4} \div 2\dfrac{5}{8} =$

Excellent! Now it's time for something new.

Level ★★★

Date / /

Name

Score /100

---

1 Change the fractions below into decimals.

3 points per question

(1) $\dfrac{7}{5} = 7 \div 5$

$=$

(2) $\dfrac{1}{8} =$

(3) $\dfrac{31}{4} =$

(4) $\dfrac{3}{100} =$

(5) $\dfrac{243}{100} =$

(6) $\dfrac{27}{1000} =$

---

2 Change the decimals below into fractions. Write the answer as either a proper fraction or a mixed number.

4 points per question

(1) $0.6 = \dfrac{\square}{10} =$

(2) $0.05 =$

(3) $0.18 =$

(4) $0.032 =$

(5) $1.2 =$

(6) $2.52 =$

(7) $3.125 =$

(8) $14.25 =$

---

3 **Add and subtract after changing the decimals into fractions.**

5 points per question

(1) $0.5 + \dfrac{1}{6} = \dfrac{\square}{2} + \dfrac{1}{6}$

$= $

(2) $0.2 + \dfrac{1}{4} =$

(3) $0.25 + \dfrac{2}{3} =$

(4) $3\dfrac{1}{2} + 2.4 = 3\dfrac{1}{2} + 2\dfrac{\square}{5}$

$= $

(5) $1\dfrac{1}{3} + 0.3 =$

(6) $\dfrac{1}{2} - 0.3 = \dfrac{1}{2} - \dfrac{\square}{10}$

$= $

(7) $\dfrac{1}{4} - 0.2 =$

(8) $0.8 - \dfrac{3}{4} =$

(9) $2\dfrac{1}{5} - 0.25 =$

(10) $2\dfrac{2}{3} - 0.4 =$

Great job! Let's keep going!

1 **Multiply after changing the decimals into fractions.**

5 points per question

(1) $0.2 \times \dfrac{5}{6} = \dfrac{\square}{5} \times \dfrac{5}{6}$

$=$

(2) $0.6 \times \dfrac{2}{3} =$

(3) $0.06 \times \dfrac{20}{21} =$

(4) $0.25 \times 3\dfrac{1}{5} = \dfrac{\square}{4} \times \dfrac{\square}{5}$

$=$

(5) $0.15 \times 40 = \dfrac{\square}{20} \times \dfrac{\square}{1}$

$=$

(6) $\dfrac{5}{28} \times 0.7 =$

(7) $3\dfrac{1}{2} \times 2.5 =$

(8) $2\dfrac{2}{3} \times 0.75 =$

(9) $5\dfrac{1}{3} \times 2.25 =$

(10) $\dfrac{4}{15} \times 1.25 =$

2 Divide after changing the decimals into fractions.

5 points per question

(1) $0.6 \div \dfrac{2}{3} = \dfrac{3}{5} \div \dfrac{2}{3}$

$= \dfrac{3}{5} \times \dfrac{3}{2}$

$=$

(2) $0.8 \div \dfrac{2}{3} =$

(3) $2.4 \div \dfrac{8}{9} =$

(4) $0.75 \div \dfrac{3}{4} =$

(5) $1.25 \div \dfrac{5}{6} =$

(6) $1\dfrac{2}{3} \div 0.5 = \dfrac{5}{3} \div \dfrac{1}{2}$

$= \dfrac{5}{3} \times \dfrac{2}{1}$

$=$

(7) $\dfrac{2}{5} \div 0.8 =$

(8) $\dfrac{3}{4} \div 0.15 =$

(9) $4\dfrac{1}{2} \div 0.18 =$

(10) $3\dfrac{3}{4} \div 1.25 =$

If you end up with an improper fraction, convert it to a mixed number for the final answer.

1 **Multiply.**

5 points per question

(1) $\dfrac{3}{4} \times \dfrac{2}{5} \times \dfrac{5}{9} = \dfrac{\overset{1}{3} \times \overset{1}{2} \times \overset{1}{5}}{\underset{2}{4} \times \underset{1}{5} \times \underset{3}{9}} = \dfrac{\square}{6}$

(6) $\dfrac{3}{8} \times \dfrac{4}{15} \times \dfrac{5}{7} =$

(2) $\dfrac{8}{9} \times \dfrac{3}{5} \times \dfrac{1}{4} =$

(7) $\dfrac{7}{10} \times \dfrac{5}{9} \times \dfrac{3}{14} =$

(3) $\dfrac{3}{4} \times 2 \times 8 =$

(8) $4 \times \dfrac{2}{7} \times \dfrac{5}{16} = \dfrac{\overset{1}{4} \times 2 \times 5}{7 \times \underset{4}{\underset{2}{16}}} =$

(4) $\dfrac{8}{9} \times \dfrac{1}{4} \times \dfrac{6}{7} =$

(9) $\dfrac{5}{6} \times \dfrac{4}{7} \times \dfrac{21}{25} =$

(5) $\dfrac{3}{5} \times \dfrac{2}{3} \times \dfrac{5}{8} =$

(10) $\dfrac{11}{18} \times \dfrac{3}{5} \times \dfrac{15}{22} =$

2 **Calculate.**

5 points per question

(1) $\dfrac{3}{7} \div \dfrac{4}{7} \times \dfrac{5}{6} = \dfrac{3 \times 7 \times 5}{7 \times 4 \times 6} =$

(6) $\dfrac{4}{5} \div \dfrac{8}{15} \times \dfrac{1}{3} =$

(2) $\dfrac{5}{7} \times \dfrac{2}{3} \div \dfrac{2}{7} =$

(7) $\dfrac{4}{5} \times \dfrac{1}{3} \div \dfrac{8}{15} =$

(3) $\dfrac{5}{6} \times \dfrac{3}{4} \div \dfrac{5}{8} =$

(8) $\dfrac{3}{7} \div \dfrac{4}{5} \times \dfrac{2}{15} =$

(4) $\dfrac{7}{8} \div \dfrac{1}{2} \times \dfrac{4}{21} =$

(9) $\dfrac{2}{7} \div \dfrac{2}{3} \div \dfrac{3}{4} =$

(5) $\dfrac{2}{9} \times \dfrac{6}{7} \div \dfrac{5}{14} =$

(10) $\dfrac{2}{5} \div \dfrac{6}{7} \div \dfrac{1}{3} =$

Well done! Let's check your score.

Three Numbers ◆Mixed Calculations

Level ★★★

Date   /   /

Name

Score

/100

1 **Calculate.**

5 points per question

(1) $4 \div \dfrac{2}{3} \div 2 = \dfrac{4}{1} \times \dfrac{3}{\square} \times \dfrac{\square}{2}$

   $=$

(2) $6 \div \dfrac{2}{3} \div \dfrac{3}{4} =$

(3) $\dfrac{4}{5} \div \dfrac{2}{3} \div \dfrac{1}{2} =$

(4) $\dfrac{7}{9} \div \dfrac{14}{15} \div \dfrac{2}{5} =$

(5) $\dfrac{7}{24} \div \dfrac{7}{8} \div \dfrac{1}{2} =$

(6) $\dfrac{3}{7} \div \dfrac{3}{8} \times \dfrac{7}{8} =$

(7) $\dfrac{3}{4} \times \dfrac{2}{3} \div 5 =$

(8) $\dfrac{3}{4} \div 5 \times \dfrac{2}{3} =$

(9) $\dfrac{8}{9} \div \dfrac{4}{5} \times 3 =$

(10) $\dfrac{8}{9} \times 3 \div \dfrac{4}{5} =$

2 **Calculate after changing the decimals into fractions.**

5 points per question

(1) $\dfrac{3}{4} \times \dfrac{3}{5} \div 0.2 =$

(2) $\dfrac{5}{12} \div 0.25 \div \dfrac{2}{3} =$

(3) $\dfrac{3}{8} \div 0.6 \times \dfrac{4}{15} =$

(4) $0.75 \times \dfrac{7}{9} \div 1\dfrac{1}{6} =$

(5) $\dfrac{5}{16} \div \dfrac{7}{8} \times 0.7 =$

(6) $\dfrac{2}{3} \times 0.6 \div 2 =$

(7) $\dfrac{8}{15} \div 4 \times 0.9 =$

(8) $\dfrac{8}{9} \div \dfrac{3}{5} \times 1.2 =$

(9) $1\dfrac{1}{6} \div 1\dfrac{2}{5} \div 1.4 =$

(10) $1.25 \div 1\dfrac{1}{8} \times 0.6 =$

Are you ready to review what you've learned?

Date / /

Name

1 **Reduce.**

2 points per question

(1) $\dfrac{20}{28} =$

(3) $\dfrac{6}{18} =$

(5) $\dfrac{12}{27} =$

(2) $\dfrac{21}{35} =$

(4) $\dfrac{45}{54} =$

(6) $\dfrac{24}{72} =$

2 **Add.**

3 points per question

(1) $\dfrac{1}{3} + \dfrac{2}{5} =$

(5) $\dfrac{3}{4} + \dfrac{3}{10} =$

(2) $\dfrac{5}{12} + \dfrac{3}{8} =$

(6) $\dfrac{9}{14} + 1\dfrac{6}{7} =$

(3) $\dfrac{1}{9} + \dfrac{7}{18} =$

(7) $2\dfrac{5}{12} + \dfrac{4}{9} =$

(4) $1\dfrac{5}{6} + \dfrac{1}{15} =$

(8) $1\dfrac{7}{10} + 2\dfrac{5}{6} =$

3 **Subtract.** 4 points per question

(1) $\dfrac{3}{4} - \dfrac{3}{8} =$

(2) $\dfrac{5}{6} - \dfrac{1}{10} =$

(3) $1\dfrac{11}{12} - \dfrac{2}{3} =$

(4) $2\dfrac{1}{14} - 1\dfrac{4}{7} =$

4 **Multiply.** 4 points per question

(1) $\dfrac{4}{9} \times \dfrac{6}{7} =$

(2) $\dfrac{5}{8} \times \dfrac{4}{5} =$

(3) $\dfrac{7}{12} \times 8 =$

(4) $\dfrac{3}{8} \times 1\dfrac{1}{5} =$

(5) $1\dfrac{1}{3} \times \dfrac{9}{10} =$

(6) $1\dfrac{2}{5} \times 1\dfrac{4}{21} =$

5 **Divide.** 4 points per question

(1) $\dfrac{5}{6} \div \dfrac{2}{3} =$

(2) $\dfrac{8}{9} \div \dfrac{3}{4} =$

(3) $1\dfrac{3}{7} \div 5 =$

(4) $4 \div \dfrac{2}{5} =$

(5) $1\dfrac{5}{9} \div \dfrac{6}{7} =$

(6) $1\dfrac{7}{15} \div 1\dfrac{2}{9} =$

Congratulations! You can add, subtract, multiply and divide positive numbers. Well done!!

1 Addition of Fractions pp 2, 3

1
(1) $\frac{4}{5}$ (6) $3\frac{2}{3}$
(2) 1 (7) $2\frac{5}{7}$
(3) $\frac{6}{7}$ (8) 2
(4) $1\frac{2}{7}$ (9) $2\frac{7}{9}$
(5) $2\frac{4}{5}$ (10) 4

2
(1) $\frac{5}{7}$ (6) $\frac{8}{9}$
(2) $1\frac{2}{9}$ (7) $4\frac{3}{7}$
(3) $2\frac{3}{5}$ (8) 4
(4) $2\frac{2}{7}$ (9) $4\frac{2}{7}$
(5) $4\frac{2}{5}$ (10) $4\frac{1}{11}$

2 Subtraction of Fractions pp 4, 5

1
(1) $\frac{3}{5}$ (6) $1\frac{2}{5}$
(2) $\frac{4}{7}$ (7) $1\frac{3}{7}$
(3) $\frac{3}{4}$ (8) $1\frac{2}{5}$
(4) $\frac{4}{5}$ (9) $2\frac{4}{9}$
(5) $2\frac{2}{7}$ (10) $2\frac{3}{5}$

2
(1) $\frac{1}{6}$ (6) $1\frac{5}{8}$
(2) $1\frac{3}{5}$ (7) $\frac{1}{7}$
(3) $\frac{5}{9}$ (8) $1\frac{4}{5}$
(4) $\frac{5}{7}$ (9) $1\frac{4}{11}$
(5) $2\frac{3}{11}$ (10) $\frac{4}{9}$

3 Mixed Review pp 6, 7

1
(1) $1\frac{1}{5}$ (6) $3\frac{3}{8}$
(2) $\frac{5}{7}$ (7) 1
(3) $3\frac{5}{6}$ (8) $3\frac{2}{7}$
(4) $3\frac{5}{9}$ (9) $4\frac{10}{11}$
(5) $2\frac{1}{11}$ (10) $4\frac{2}{9}$

2
(1) $\frac{5}{7}$ (6) $1\frac{2}{3}$
(2) $\frac{5}{9}$ (7) $\frac{5}{11}$
(3) 0 (8) $1\frac{3}{7}$
(4) $1\frac{3}{11}$ (9) $\frac{5}{9}$
(5) $\frac{3}{7}$ (10) $1\frac{7}{11}$

Advice
If you scored over 85 on this section, review your mistakes and move on to the next section.
If you scored between 75 and 84 on this section, review the beginning of this book before moving on.
If you scored less than 74 on this section, it might be a good idea to go back to our "Grade 5 Decimals & Fractions" book and do an extended review of fractions.

4 Reduction pp 8, 9

1
(1) $\frac{1}{3}$ (5) $\frac{4}{5}$ (9) $\frac{9}{10}$
(2) $\frac{3}{4}$ (6) $\frac{2}{7}$ (10) $\frac{8}{13}$
(3) $\frac{1}{2}$ (7) $\frac{3}{8}$
(4) $\frac{2}{3}$ (8) $\frac{5}{9}$

2
(1) $\frac{1}{2}$ (5) $\frac{3}{5}$ (9) $\frac{4}{9}$
(2) $\frac{1}{3}$ (6) $\frac{4}{5}$ (10) $\frac{8}{9}$
(3) $\frac{3}{4}$ (7) $\frac{3}{7}$
(4) $\frac{2}{5}$ (8) $\frac{7}{8}$

3
(1) $\frac{1}{3}$ (8) $\frac{7}{8}$ (15) $\frac{5}{8}$
(2) $\frac{1}{2}$ (9) $\frac{5}{9}$ (16) $\frac{3}{13}$
(3) $\frac{2}{3}$ (10) $\frac{5}{6}$ (17) $\frac{2}{9}$
(4) $\frac{3}{4}$ (11) $\frac{1}{7}$ (18) $\frac{4}{15}$
(5) $\frac{3}{5}$ (12) $\frac{6}{7}$ (19) $\frac{3}{10}$
(6) $\frac{5}{6}$ (13) $\frac{4}{11}$ (20) $\frac{7}{10}$
(7) $\frac{2}{5}$ (14) $\frac{5}{12}$

5 Reduction pp 10, 11

1
(1) $\frac{2}{3}$ (5) $\frac{1}{4}$ (9) $\frac{5}{6}$
(2) $\frac{1}{2}$ (6) $\frac{7}{12}$ (10) $\frac{7}{8}$
(3) $\frac{5}{6}$ (7) $\frac{3}{5}$
(4) $\frac{2}{3}$ (8) $\frac{7}{15}$

2
(1) $\frac{1}{2}$ (5) $\frac{1}{7}$ (9) $\frac{4}{5}$
(2) $\frac{2}{3}$ (6) $\frac{4}{7}$ (10) $\frac{7}{9}$
(3) $\frac{1}{3}$ (7) $\frac{1}{5}$
(4) $\frac{3}{4}$ (8) $\frac{2}{5}$

3
(1) $\frac{3}{4}$ (5) $\frac{1}{2}$ (9) $\frac{3}{4}$
(2) $\frac{2}{5}$ (6) $\frac{7}{9}$ (10) $\frac{4}{5}$
(3) $\frac{5}{6}$ (7) $\frac{2}{3}$
(4) $\frac{3}{7}$ (8) $\frac{8}{11}$

4
(1) $\frac{3}{5}$ (5) $\frac{3}{8}$ (9) $\frac{3}{5}$
(2) $\frac{2}{7}$ (6) $\frac{7}{8}$ (10) $\frac{5}{6}$
(3) $\frac{1}{3}$ (7) $\frac{1}{4}$
(4) $\frac{5}{7}$ (8) $\frac{2}{5}$

6 Reduction pp 12, 13

1
(1) $\frac{1}{2}$ (5) $\frac{1}{5}$ (9) $\frac{4}{5}$
(2) $\frac{2}{5}$ (6) $\frac{2}{5}$ (10) $\frac{5}{6}$
(3) $\frac{1}{4}$ (7) $\frac{3}{7}$
(4) $\frac{1}{7}$ (8) $\frac{5}{7}$

2
(1) $\frac{3}{5}$ (5) $\frac{14}{17}$ (9) $\frac{4}{9}$
(2) $\frac{7}{11}$ (6) $\frac{1}{19}$ (10) $\frac{2}{7}$
(3) $\frac{7}{8}$ (7) $\frac{9}{13}$
(4) $\frac{11}{13}$ (8) $\frac{3}{8}$

3
(1) $\frac{2}{3}$ (5) $\frac{4}{5}$ (9) $\frac{3}{4}$
(2) $\frac{1}{2}$ (6) $\frac{1}{3}$ (10) $\frac{3}{5}$
(3) $\frac{1}{3}$ (7) $\frac{1}{2}$
(4) $\frac{3}{4}$ (8) $\frac{2}{3}$

4
(1) $\frac{1}{4}$ (5) $\frac{2}{3}$ (9) $\frac{3}{4}$
(2) $\frac{1}{2}$ (6) $\frac{2}{7}$ (10) $\frac{4}{9}$
(3) $\frac{4}{5}$ (7) $\frac{1}{4}$
(4) $\frac{1}{3}$ (8) $\frac{5}{8}$

7 Reduction
pp 14, 15

1
(1) $\frac{3}{4}$ (8) $\frac{1}{2}$ (15) $\frac{7}{10}$
(2) $\frac{1}{3}$ (9) $\frac{1}{3}$ (16) $\frac{4}{5}$
(3) $\frac{4}{7}$ (10) $\frac{2}{3}$ (17) $\frac{1}{6}$
(4) $\frac{4}{5}$ (11) $\frac{1}{4}$ (18) $\frac{4}{9}$
(5) $\frac{3}{4}$ (12) $\frac{3}{4}$ (19) $\frac{2}{7}$
(6) $\frac{2}{5}$ (13) $\frac{7}{10}$ (20) $\frac{5}{12}$
(7) $\frac{4}{5}$ (14) $\frac{5}{6}$

2
(1) $\frac{1}{4}$ (8) $\frac{1}{3}$ (15) $\frac{1}{4}$
(2) $\frac{1}{3}$ (9) $\frac{1}{3}$ (16) $\frac{1}{5}$
(3) $\frac{1}{3}$ (10) $\frac{2}{3}$ (17) $\frac{1}{4}$
(4) $\frac{1}{2}$ (11) $\frac{5}{7}$ (18) $\frac{1}{3}$
(5) $\frac{1}{3}$ (12) $\frac{2}{9}$ (19) $\frac{1}{2}$
(6) $\frac{2}{3}$ (13) $\frac{1}{3}$ (20) $\frac{2}{3}$
(7) $\frac{1}{4}$ (14) $\frac{1}{7}$

8 Reduction
pp 16, 17

1
(1) 6
(2) 9
(3) 6

2
(1) 5
(2) 6
(3) 10

3
(1) 6
(2) 10

4
(1) 4   (3) 6
(2) 6   (4) 8

5
(1) 4, $\frac{3}{5}$
(2) 4, $\frac{5}{6}$
(3) 6, $\frac{3}{4}$
(4) 6, $\frac{2}{5}$
(5) 15, $\frac{1}{2}$
(6) 9, $\frac{2}{3}$
(7) 8, $\frac{3}{4}$
(8) 9, $\frac{3}{4}$
(9) 12, $\frac{3}{4}$
(10) 15, $\frac{3}{4}$

9 Reduction
pp 18, 19

1
(1) 6
(2) 10
(3) 6
(4) 30
(5) 12
(6) 7
(7) 8
(8) 27
(9) 12
(10) 18

2
(1) $\frac{1}{3}$ (8) $\frac{4}{7}$ (15) $\frac{1}{3}$
(2) $\frac{1}{4}$ (9) $\frac{4}{5}$ (16) $\frac{5}{12}$
(3) $\frac{3}{4}$ (10) $\frac{5}{6}$ (17) $\frac{11}{17}$
(4) $\frac{1}{3}$ (11) $\frac{1}{3}$ (18) $\frac{2}{3}$
(5) $\frac{2}{3}$ (12) $\frac{3}{4}$ (19) $\frac{5}{8}$
(6) $\frac{2}{3}$ (13) $\frac{2}{5}$ (20) $\frac{3}{11}$
(7) $\frac{1}{2}$ (14) $\frac{2}{7}$

Advice
When you can't find the GCF because the numbers are very large, try solving the problem by using the method shown in the example.

10 Addition of Fractions
pp 20, 21

1
(1) $\frac{\boxed{3}}{6}$ (8) $\frac{\boxed{15}}{24}$ (15) $\frac{12}{36}$
(2) $\frac{\boxed{4}}{12}$ (9) $\frac{\boxed{4}}{18}$ (16) $\frac{32}{56}$
(3) $\frac{\boxed{2}}{8}$ (10) $\frac{\boxed{15}}{27}$ (17) $\frac{30}{80}$
(4) $\frac{\boxed{3}}{15}$ (11) $\frac{4}{8}$ (18) $\frac{63}{72}$
(5) $\frac{\boxed{8}}{20}$ (12) $\frac{14}{21}$ (19) $\frac{9}{81}$
(6) $\frac{\boxed{5}}{35}$ (13) $\frac{21}{28}$ (20) $\frac{28}{63}$
(7) $\frac{\boxed{18}}{42}$ (14) $\frac{24}{40}$

2
(1) $\frac{3}{8}+\frac{1}{4}=\frac{3}{8}+\frac{\boxed{2}}{8}=\frac{5}{8}$ (6) $\frac{1}{6}+\frac{2}{3}=\frac{1}{6}+\frac{4}{6}=\frac{5}{6}$
(2) $\frac{5}{8}+\frac{1}{4}=\frac{\boxed{5}}{8}+\frac{\boxed{2}}{8}=\frac{7}{8}$ (7) $\frac{1}{10}+\frac{1}{5}=\frac{1}{10}+\frac{2}{10}=\frac{3}{10}$
(3) $\frac{1}{9}+\frac{1}{3}=\frac{1}{9}+\frac{\boxed{3}}{9}=\frac{4}{9}$ (8) $\frac{2}{5}+\frac{3}{10}=\frac{4}{10}+\frac{3}{10}=\frac{7}{10}$
(4) $\frac{4}{9}+\frac{1}{3}=\frac{4}{9}+\frac{3}{9}=\frac{7}{9}$ (9) $\frac{1}{12}+\frac{1}{3}=\frac{1}{12}+\frac{4}{12}=\frac{5}{12}$
(5) $\frac{1}{8}+\frac{1}{2}=\frac{1}{8}+\frac{4}{8}=\frac{5}{8}$ (10) $\frac{1}{3}+\frac{7}{12}=\frac{4}{12}+\frac{7}{12}=\frac{11}{12}$

11 Addition of Fractions
pp 22, 23

1
(1) $\frac{1}{12}+\frac{1}{6}=\frac{\boxed{1}}{12}+\frac{\boxed{2}}{12}$
$=\frac{\boxed{3}}{12}=\frac{\boxed{1}}{4}$
(6) $\frac{1}{18}+\frac{1}{6}=\frac{1}{18}+\frac{3}{18}$
$=\frac{4}{18}=\frac{2}{9}$
(2) $\frac{3}{4}$ (7) $\frac{4}{9}$
(3) $\frac{1}{3}$ (8) $\frac{5}{9}$
(4) $\frac{2}{3}$ (9) $\frac{1}{6}$
(5) $\frac{5}{6}$ (10) $\frac{1}{2}$

2
(1) $\frac{1}{2}+\frac{5}{8}=\frac{\boxed{4}}{8}+\frac{\boxed{5}}{8}$
$=\frac{\boxed{9}}{8}=1\frac{\boxed{1}}{8}$
(6) $\frac{5}{6}+\frac{5}{24}=\frac{20}{24}+\frac{5}{24}$
$=\frac{25}{24}=1\frac{1}{24}$
(2) $1\frac{1}{9}$ (7) $1\frac{1}{4}$
(3) $1\frac{1}{6}$ (8) $1\frac{3}{8}$
(4) $1\frac{1}{8}$ (9) $1\frac{4}{9}$
(5) $1\frac{1}{10}$ (10) $1\frac{3}{8}$

(12) Addition of Fractions

pp 24, 25

(1) 24, 30, 36, 42, 48, 54

(2) 24, 32, 40, 48, 56

(3) 18, 27, 36, 45, 54

(4) 24, 48, 72, 96

(5) 18, 36, 54, 72

(6) 12, 24, 36, 48

(7) (1) 18
(2) 12

(8) (1) 24   (2) 36

(9) (1) 12   (3) 45
(2) 30   (4) 20

(10) (1) $\dfrac{1}{6}=\dfrac{\boxed{3}}{18}$, $\dfrac{1}{9}=\dfrac{\boxed{2}}{18}$
　　$\dfrac{1}{6}+\dfrac{1}{9}=\dfrac{\boxed{3}}{18}+\dfrac{\boxed{2}}{18}$
　　　　　$=\dfrac{\boxed{5}}{18}$

(2) $\dfrac{1}{6}+\dfrac{4}{9}=\dfrac{\boxed{3}}{18}+\dfrac{\boxed{8}}{18}$
　　　　$=\dfrac{\boxed{11}}{18}$

(11) (1) 24

(2) $\dfrac{1}{6}+\dfrac{1}{8}=\dfrac{\boxed{4}}{24}+\dfrac{\boxed{3}}{24}$
　　　$=\dfrac{\boxed{7}}{24}$

(3) $\dfrac{1}{6}+\dfrac{5}{8}=\dfrac{\boxed{4}}{24}+\dfrac{\boxed{15}}{24}$
　　　$=\dfrac{\boxed{19}}{24}$

(4) $\dfrac{5}{6}+\dfrac{1}{8}=\dfrac{\boxed{20}}{24}+\dfrac{3}{24}$
　　　$=\dfrac{\boxed{23}}{24}$

(13) Addition of Fractions

pp 26, 27

(1) (1) 12, $\dfrac{1}{4}+\dfrac{1}{6}=\dfrac{\boxed{3}}{12}+\dfrac{\boxed{2}}{12}$
　　　　　$=\dfrac{5}{12}$

(2) 20, $\dfrac{11}{20}$

(3) 40, $\dfrac{17}{40}$

(4) 24, $\dfrac{11}{24}$

(5) 36, $\dfrac{7}{36}$

(6) 30, $\dfrac{13}{30}$

(2) (1) 12   (7) 56
(2) 36   (8) 40
(3) 28   (9) 45
(4) 44   (10) 30
(5) 60   (11) 70
(6) 60   (12) 90

(3)

(1) $\dfrac{3}{4}+\dfrac{1}{6}=\dfrac{\boxed{9}}{12}+\dfrac{\boxed{2}}{12}=\dfrac{11}{12}$ (6) $\dfrac{11}{45}$

(2) $\dfrac{25}{36}$ (7) $\dfrac{13}{30}$

(3) $\dfrac{9}{28}$

(4) $\dfrac{43}{60}$

(5) $\dfrac{41}{56}$

(14) Addition of Fractions

pp 28, 29

(1) (1) $\dfrac{5}{6}+\dfrac{1}{10}=\dfrac{\boxed{25}}{30}+\dfrac{\boxed{3}}{30}=\dfrac{\boxed{28}}{30}=\dfrac{\boxed{14}}{15}$ (6) $\dfrac{9}{10}$

(2) $\dfrac{3}{10}$ (7) $\dfrac{11}{12}$

(3) $\dfrac{13}{24}$ (8) $\dfrac{13}{14}$

(4) $\dfrac{11}{21}$ (9) $\dfrac{19}{20}$

(5) $\dfrac{5}{6}$ (10) $\dfrac{25}{42}$

(2) (1) $\dfrac{1}{4}+\dfrac{5}{6}=\dfrac{\boxed{3}}{12}+\dfrac{\boxed{10}}{12}=\dfrac{\boxed{13}}{12}=1\dfrac{\boxed{1}}{12}$ (6) $1\dfrac{1}{14}$

(2) $1\dfrac{1}{20}$ (7) $1\dfrac{1}{15}$

(3) $1\dfrac{5}{24}$ (8) $1\dfrac{5}{21}$

(4) $1\dfrac{5}{24}$ (9) $1\dfrac{11}{42}$

(5) $1\dfrac{7}{20}$ (10) $1\dfrac{5}{72}$

(15) Addition of Fractions

pp 30, 31

(1) (1) $\dfrac{5}{6}+\dfrac{4}{15}=\dfrac{\boxed{25}}{30}+\dfrac{\boxed{8}}{30}$ (6) $1\dfrac{1}{5}$
　　　$=\dfrac{\boxed{33}}{30}=\dfrac{\boxed{11}}{10}=1\dfrac{\boxed{1}}{10}$

(2) $1\dfrac{1}{6}$ (7) $1\dfrac{1}{2}$

(3) $1\dfrac{1}{3}$ (8) $1\dfrac{1}{4}$

(4) $1\dfrac{1}{6}$ (9) $1\dfrac{8}{15}$

(5) $1\dfrac{1}{3}$ (10) $\dfrac{1}{2}$

(2) (1) $\dfrac{8}{9}$ (6) $\dfrac{9}{10}$

(2) $\dfrac{4}{5}$ (7) $1\dfrac{1}{6}$

(3) $1\dfrac{1}{20}$ (8) $1\dfrac{1}{18}$

(4) $1\dfrac{1}{4}$ (9) $1\dfrac{10}{21}$

(5) $1\dfrac{11}{24}$ (10) $1\dfrac{1}{14}$

16) Addition of Fractions

1) (1) 48 (6) 120
(2) 40 (7) 96
(3) 60 (8) 120
(4) 18 (9) 240
(5) 80 (10) 252

2) (1) $\dfrac{1}{8}+\dfrac{1}{12}=\dfrac{\boxed{3}}{24}+\dfrac{\boxed{2}}{24}=\dfrac{5}{24}$ (6) $\dfrac{19}{20}$
(2) $\dfrac{19}{40}$ (7) $\dfrac{49}{75}$
(3) $\dfrac{29}{48}$ (8) $\dfrac{19}{80}$
(4) $\dfrac{31}{36}$ (9) $\dfrac{31}{96}$
(5) $\dfrac{23}{30}$ (10) $\dfrac{11}{40}$

Advice
You can always find the GCF by searching through the multiples of the larger number until you find one that fits for both numbers. However, with larger numbers, using the method shown in the example will be much easier.

17) Addition of Fractions
pp 34,35

1) (1) $\dfrac{2}{3}$ (6) $\dfrac{7}{30}$
(2) $\dfrac{37}{84}$ (7) $\dfrac{9}{20}$
(3) $\dfrac{5}{42}$ (8) $\dfrac{4}{45}$
(4) $\dfrac{31}{45}$ (9) $\dfrac{7}{12}$
(5) $\dfrac{3}{5}$ (10) $\dfrac{33}{40}$

2) (1) $1\dfrac{2}{9}$ (6) $1\dfrac{7}{48}$
(2) $1\dfrac{1}{36}$ (7) $1\dfrac{1}{4}$
(3) $1\dfrac{1}{4}$ (8) $1\dfrac{9}{50}$
(4) $1\dfrac{1}{15}$ (9) $1\dfrac{1}{10}$
(5) $1\dfrac{1}{6}$ (10) $1\dfrac{4}{45}$

18) Addition of Fractions
pp 36,37

1) (1) $1\dfrac{1}{2}+2\dfrac{1}{3}=1\dfrac{\boxed{3}}{6}+2\dfrac{\boxed{2}}{6}=3\dfrac{\boxed{5}}{6}$ (6) $2\dfrac{7}{8}$
(2) $2\dfrac{1}{2}+1\dfrac{1}{4}=2\dfrac{2}{4}+1\dfrac{1}{4}=3\dfrac{3}{4}$ (7) $1\dfrac{11}{15}$
(3) $2\dfrac{8}{15}$ (8) $2\dfrac{11}{15}$
(4) $3\dfrac{7}{12}$ (9) $3\dfrac{13}{16}$
(5) $2\dfrac{1}{6}+1\dfrac{1}{8}=2\dfrac{4}{24}+1\dfrac{3}{24}=3\dfrac{7}{24}$ (10) $5\dfrac{35}{36}$

2) (1) $1\dfrac{1}{3}+2\dfrac{3}{4}=1\dfrac{\boxed{4}}{12}+2\dfrac{\boxed{9}}{12}=3\dfrac{\boxed{13}}{12}=4\dfrac{\boxed{1}}{12}$ (6) $3\dfrac{1}{6}$
(2) $2\dfrac{1}{3}+1\dfrac{5}{6}=2\dfrac{2}{6}+1\dfrac{5}{6}=3\dfrac{7}{6}=4\dfrac{1}{6}$ (7) $2\dfrac{7}{15}$
(3) $2\dfrac{3}{4}+2\dfrac{5}{9}=2\dfrac{27}{36}+2\dfrac{20}{36}=4\dfrac{47}{36}=5\dfrac{11}{36}$ (8) $3\dfrac{7}{12}$
(4) $5\dfrac{1}{18}$ (9) $6\dfrac{1}{24}$
(5) $3\dfrac{5}{12}$ (10) $4\dfrac{5}{18}$

19) Addition of Fractions
pp 38,39

1) (1) $1\dfrac{1}{6}+2\dfrac{1}{3}=1\dfrac{1}{6}+2\dfrac{\boxed{2}}{6}=3\dfrac{\boxed{3}}{6}=3\dfrac{1}{2}$
(2) $2\dfrac{1}{4}+1\dfrac{5}{12}=2\dfrac{3}{12}+1\dfrac{5}{12}=3\dfrac{8}{12}=3\dfrac{2}{3}$
(3) $1\dfrac{4}{9}+3\dfrac{7}{18}=1\dfrac{8}{18}+3\dfrac{7}{18}=4\dfrac{15}{18}=4\dfrac{5}{6}$
(4) $2\dfrac{1}{6}+1\dfrac{3}{10}=2\dfrac{5}{30}+1\dfrac{9}{30}=3\dfrac{14}{30}=3\dfrac{7}{15}$
(5) $\dfrac{3}{4}+3\dfrac{1}{20}=\dfrac{15}{20}+3\dfrac{1}{20}=3\dfrac{16}{20}=3\dfrac{4}{5}$
(6) $1\dfrac{7}{15}+\dfrac{5}{6}=1\dfrac{14}{30}+\dfrac{25}{30}=1\dfrac{39}{30}=2\dfrac{9}{30}=2\dfrac{3}{10}$
$\left(\text{or}=1\dfrac{39}{30}=1\dfrac{13}{10}=2\dfrac{3}{10}\right)$
(7) $1\dfrac{11}{12}$
(8) $4\dfrac{1}{15}$
(9) $6\dfrac{1}{4}$
(10) $2\dfrac{11}{15}+1\dfrac{1}{6}=2\dfrac{22}{30}+1\dfrac{5}{30}=3\dfrac{27}{30}=3\dfrac{9}{10}$

2) (1) $4\dfrac{2}{3}$ (6) $3\dfrac{11}{12}$
(2) $2\dfrac{1}{12}$ (7) $3\dfrac{1}{7}$
(3) $3\dfrac{1}{10}$ (8) $3\dfrac{1}{10}$
(4) $3\dfrac{7}{20}$ (9) $3\dfrac{2}{21}$
(5) $5\dfrac{7}{12}$ (10) $3\dfrac{23}{24}$

Advice
If you can reduce an answer, reduce it.

20) Subtraction of Fractions
pp 40,41

1) (1) $\dfrac{1}{4}-\dfrac{1}{8}=\dfrac{\boxed{2}}{8}-\dfrac{1}{8}=\dfrac{1}{8}$ (6) $\dfrac{5}{9}$
(2) $\dfrac{5}{8}$ (7) $\dfrac{4}{9}$
(3) $\dfrac{3}{8}$ (8) $\dfrac{3}{8}$
(4) $\dfrac{1}{8}$ (9) $\dfrac{1}{8}$
(5) $\dfrac{2}{9}$ (10) $\dfrac{1}{4}$

2) (1) $\dfrac{1}{6}$ (6) $\dfrac{3}{10}$
(2) $\dfrac{1}{10}$ (7) $\dfrac{4}{21}$
(3) $\dfrac{3}{10}$ (8) $\dfrac{1}{20}$
(4) $\dfrac{1}{2}-\dfrac{1}{5}=\dfrac{\boxed{5}}{10}-\dfrac{\boxed{2}}{10}=\dfrac{3}{10}$ (9) $\dfrac{2}{15}$
(5) $\dfrac{1}{10}$ (10) $\dfrac{1}{15}$

21 Subtraction of Fractions pp 42,43

1
(1) $\frac{2}{3} - \frac{1}{6} = \frac{\boxed{4}}{6} - \frac{1}{6} = \frac{\boxed{3}}{6} = \frac{1}{2}$ (6) $\frac{1}{6}$
(2) $\frac{1}{2} - \frac{1}{6} = \frac{3}{6} - \frac{1}{6} = \frac{2}{6} = \frac{1}{3}$ (7) $\frac{1}{3}$
(3) $\frac{1}{2} - \frac{3}{10} = \frac{5}{10} - \frac{3}{10} = \frac{2}{10} = \frac{1}{5}$ (8) $\frac{1}{4}$
(4) $\frac{3}{5} - \frac{1}{10} = \frac{6}{10} - \frac{1}{10} = \frac{5}{10} = \frac{1}{2}$ (9) $\frac{1}{3}$
(5) $\frac{4}{5} - \frac{3}{10} = \frac{8}{10} - \frac{3}{10} = \frac{5}{10} = \frac{1}{2}$ (10) $\frac{2}{9}$

2
(1) $\frac{3}{4} - \frac{1}{6} = \frac{\boxed{9}}{12} - \frac{\boxed{2}}{12} = \frac{7}{12}$ (6) $\frac{5}{24}$
(2) $\frac{1}{6} - \frac{1}{8} = \frac{4}{24} - \frac{3}{24} = \frac{1}{24}$ (7) $\frac{5}{6}$
(3) $\frac{5}{6} - \frac{2}{9} = \frac{15}{18} - \frac{4}{18} = \frac{11}{18}$ (8) $\frac{8}{15}$
(4) $\frac{5}{6} - \frac{1}{10} = \frac{25}{30} - \frac{3}{30} = \frac{22}{30} = \frac{11}{15}$ (9) $\frac{2}{35}$
(5) $\frac{5}{6} - \frac{3}{10} = \frac{25}{30} - \frac{9}{30} = \frac{16}{30} = \frac{8}{15}$ (10) $\frac{4}{45}$

22 Subtraction of Fractions pp 44,45

1
(1) $\frac{5}{4} - \frac{3}{8} = \frac{\boxed{10}}{8} - \frac{3}{8} = \frac{7}{8}$ (6) $\frac{4}{3} - \frac{2}{5} = \frac{\boxed{20}}{15} - \frac{\boxed{6}}{15} = \frac{14}{15}$
(2) $\frac{5}{4} - \frac{5}{8} = \frac{10}{8} - \frac{5}{8} = \frac{5}{8}$ (7) $\frac{7}{5} - \frac{1}{2} = \frac{14}{10} - \frac{5}{10} = \frac{9}{10}$
(3) $\frac{3}{2} - \frac{5}{8} = \frac{12}{8} - \frac{5}{8} = \frac{7}{8}$ (8) $\frac{7}{4} - \frac{5}{6} = \frac{21}{12} - \frac{10}{12} = \frac{11}{12}$
(4) $\frac{9}{8} - \frac{1}{4} = \frac{9}{8} - \frac{2}{8} = \frac{7}{8}$ (9) $\frac{7}{6} - \frac{5}{8} = \frac{28}{24} - \frac{15}{24} = \frac{13}{24}$
(5) $\frac{7}{6} - \frac{1}{3} = \frac{7}{6} - \frac{2}{6} = \frac{5}{6}$ (10) $\frac{10}{9} - \frac{5}{6} = \frac{20}{18} - \frac{15}{18} = \frac{5}{18}$

2
(1) $\frac{4}{3} - \frac{5}{6} = \frac{\boxed{8}}{6} - \frac{5}{6} = \frac{\boxed{3}}{6} = \frac{1}{2}$ (6) $\frac{2}{5}$
(2) $\frac{3}{2} - \frac{7}{10} = \frac{15}{10} - \frac{7}{10} = \frac{8}{10} = \frac{4}{5}$ (7) $\frac{13}{15}$
(3) $\frac{1}{2}$ (8) $\frac{3}{10}$
(4) $\frac{3}{4}$ (9) $\frac{5}{6}$
(5) $\frac{5}{6}$ (10) $\frac{5}{6}$

23 Subtraction of Fractions pp 46,47

1
(1) $2\frac{1}{2} - 1\frac{1}{3} = 2\frac{\boxed{3}}{6} - 1\frac{\boxed{2}}{6} = 1\frac{\boxed{1}}{6}$ (6) $1\frac{1}{4}$
(2) $3\frac{1}{3} - 2\frac{1}{4} = 3\frac{\boxed{4}}{12} - 2\frac{\boxed{3}}{12} = 1\frac{1}{12}$ (7) $2\frac{4}{21}$
(3) $2\frac{3}{5} - \frac{3}{10} = 2\frac{6}{10} - \frac{3}{10} = 2\frac{3}{10}$ (8) $2\frac{13}{36}$
(4) $3\frac{4}{9}$ (9) $1\frac{1}{12}$
(5) $4\frac{5}{12} - 1\frac{3}{8} = 4\frac{10}{24} - 1\frac{9}{24} = 3\frac{1}{24}$ (10) $1\frac{5}{24}$

2
(1) $3\frac{1}{4} - 1\frac{2}{3} = 3\frac{\boxed{3}}{12} - 1\frac{\boxed{8}}{12}$ (6) $1\frac{1}{5} - \frac{5}{6} = 1\frac{6}{30} - \frac{25}{30}$
$= 2\frac{\boxed{15}}{12} - 1\frac{8}{12}$ $\quad = \frac{36}{30} - \frac{25}{30}$
$= 1\frac{7}{12}$ $\quad = \frac{11}{30}$

(2) $4\frac{1}{6} - 2\frac{8}{9} = 4\frac{\boxed{3}}{18} - 2\frac{\boxed{16}}{18}$ (7) $1\frac{8}{9}$
$= 3\frac{21}{18} - 2\frac{16}{18}$
$= 1\frac{5}{18}$

(3) $4\frac{1}{3} - 1\frac{2}{5} = 4\frac{5}{15} - 1\frac{6}{15}$ (8) $\frac{11}{20}$
$= 3\frac{20}{15} - 1\frac{6}{15}$
$= 2\frac{14}{15}$

(4) $1\frac{3}{4}$ (9) $\frac{19}{24}$
(5) $2\frac{17}{21}$ (10) $2\frac{13}{14}$

24 Subtraction of Fractions pp 48,49

1
(1) $2\frac{2}{3} - 1\frac{1}{6} = 2\frac{\boxed{4}}{6} - 1\frac{1}{6}$ (6) $3\frac{3}{10} - 1\frac{4}{5} = 3\frac{3}{10} - 1\frac{\boxed{8}}{10}$
$= 1\frac{\boxed{3}}{6} = 1\frac{1}{2}$ $\quad = 2\frac{\boxed{13}}{10} - 1\frac{8}{10}$
$\quad = 1\frac{\boxed{5}}{10} = 1\frac{1}{2}$

(2) $3\frac{7}{12} - 1\frac{1}{3} = 3\frac{7}{12} - 1\frac{4}{12}$ (7) $4\frac{1}{6} - 2\frac{2}{3} = 4\frac{1}{6} - 2\frac{4}{6}$
$= 2\frac{3}{12} = 2\frac{1}{4}$ $\quad = 3\frac{7}{6} - 2\frac{4}{6}$
$\quad = 1\frac{3}{6} = 1\frac{1}{2}$

(3) $1\frac{1}{6} - \frac{1}{10} = 1\frac{5}{30} - \frac{3}{30}$ (8) $3\frac{1}{10} - 1\frac{5}{6} = 3\frac{3}{30} - 1\frac{25}{30}$
$= 1\frac{2}{30} = 1\frac{1}{15}$ $\quad = 2\frac{33}{30} - 1\frac{25}{30}$
$\quad = 1\frac{8}{30} = 1\frac{4}{15}$

(4) $2\frac{1}{4}$ (9) $1\frac{5}{6}$
(5) $1\frac{1}{2}$ (10) $\frac{5}{6}$

2
(1) $\frac{1}{6}$ (6) $\frac{1}{15}$
(2) $\frac{7}{12}$ (7) $1\frac{1}{3}$
(3) $\frac{11}{12}$ (8) $1\frac{5}{9}$
(4) $1\frac{3}{4}$ (9) $2\frac{4}{5}$
(5) $2\frac{1}{14}$ (10) $\frac{2}{3}$

25 Three Fractions pp 50, 51

1
(1) $\frac{1}{2}+\frac{1}{3}+\frac{1}{7}=\boxed{\frac{21}{42}}+\boxed{\frac{14}{42}}+\boxed{\frac{6}{42}}=\frac{41}{42}$
(2) $\frac{1}{2}+\frac{1}{5}+\frac{1}{7}=\frac{35}{70}+\frac{14}{70}+\frac{10}{70}=\frac{59}{70}$
(3) $\frac{73}{90}$
(4) $\frac{1}{2}+\frac{1}{5}+\frac{4}{9}=\boxed{\frac{45}{90}}+\boxed{\frac{18}{90}}+\boxed{\frac{40}{90}}=\boxed{\frac{103}{90}}=1\boxed{\frac{13}{90}}$
(5) $1\frac{23}{70}$

(6) $1\frac{1}{30}$
(7) $1\frac{29}{30}$
(8) $\frac{47}{60}$
(9) $1\frac{29}{60}$
(10) $2\frac{13}{60}$

2
(1) (12)
  (12), $\boxed{36}$
(2) (18)
  (18), $\boxed{36}$
(3) (36)
  (36), $\boxed{36}$

3
(1) 12   (6) 24   (11) 36
(2) 18   (7) 60   (12) 28
(3) 12   (8) 30   (13) 90
(4) 28   (9) 24   (14) 24
(5) 60   (10) 60

26 Three Fractions pp 52, 53

1
(1) $\frac{1}{2}+\frac{1}{3}+\frac{1}{4}=\boxed{\frac{6}{12}}+\boxed{\frac{4}{12}}+\boxed{\frac{3}{12}}=\boxed{\frac{13}{12}}=1\boxed{\frac{1}{12}}$
(2) $\frac{1}{2}+\frac{1}{3}+\frac{1}{8}=\frac{12}{24}+\frac{8}{24}+\frac{3}{24}=\frac{23}{24}$
(3) $\frac{17}{20}$
(4) $\frac{33}{40}$
(5) $\frac{17}{24}$

(6) $1\frac{2}{3}$
(7) $1\frac{5}{12}$
(8) $1\frac{5}{12}$
(9) $1\frac{19}{36}$
(10) $1\frac{3}{8}$

2
(1) $\frac{1}{2}+\frac{1}{3}-\frac{1}{4}=\boxed{\frac{6}{12}}+\boxed{\frac{4}{12}}-\boxed{\frac{3}{12}}=\boxed{\frac{7}{12}}$
(2) $\frac{23}{60}$
(3) $\frac{1}{3}+\frac{3}{4}-\frac{5}{6}=\boxed{\frac{4}{12}}+\boxed{\frac{9}{12}}-\boxed{\frac{10}{12}}=\boxed{\frac{3}{12}}=\frac{1}{4}$
(4) $\frac{7}{30}$
(5) $\frac{1}{24}$

(6) $\frac{5}{24}$
(7) $\frac{5}{24}$
(8) $\frac{17}{24}$
(9) $\frac{59}{72}$
(10) $\frac{17}{36}$

27 Multiplication of Fractions pp 54, 55

1
(1) $\frac{2}{3}\times\frac{4}{7}=\frac{2\times4}{3\times7}=\boxed{\frac{8}{21}}$
(2) $\frac{3}{5}\times\frac{1}{2}=\frac{3\times1}{5\times2}=\frac{3}{10}$
(3) $\frac{3}{20}$
(4) $\frac{5}{24}$
(5) $\frac{5}{21}$

(6) $\frac{2}{15}$
(7) $\frac{3}{20}$
(8) $\frac{9}{28}$
(9) $\frac{6}{35}$
(10) $\frac{9}{40}$

2
(1) $\frac{6}{35}$ (6) $\frac{25}{42}$
(2) $\frac{12}{35}$ (7) $\frac{35}{54}$
(3) $\frac{9}{56}$ (8) $\frac{8}{63}$
(4) $\frac{5}{42}$ (9) $\frac{15}{56}$
(5) $\frac{5}{48}$ (10) $\frac{35}{72}$

28 Multiplication of Fractions pp 56, 57

1
(1) $\frac{3}{4}\times\frac{5}{6}=\frac{3\times5}{4\times6}=\boxed{\frac{5}{8}}$
(2) $\frac{2}{3}\times\frac{1}{4}=\frac{2\times1}{3\times4}=\frac{1}{6}$
(3) $\frac{3}{10}$
(4) $\frac{1}{10}$
(5) $\frac{2}{5}$

(6) $\frac{3}{5}$
(7) $\frac{4}{7}$
(8) $\frac{4}{7}$
(9) $\frac{10}{21}$
(10) $\frac{3}{14}$

2
(1) $\frac{3}{20}$ (6) $\frac{4}{9}$
(2) $\frac{3}{10}$ (7) $\frac{3}{20}$
(3) $\frac{5}{12}$ (8) $\frac{9}{35}$
(4) $\frac{15}{28}$ (9) $\frac{14}{27}$
(5) $\frac{5}{8}$ (10) $\frac{10}{33}$

29 Multiplication of Fractions pp 58, 59

1
(1) $\frac{2}{3}\times\frac{3}{4}=\frac{\boxed{1}2}{3}\times\frac{3}{4\boxed{2}}=\frac{1}{2}$
(2) $\frac{1}{3}$
(3) $\frac{3}{4}$
(4) $\frac{1}{4}$

(5) $\frac{2}{3}$
(6) $\frac{1}{3}$
(7) $\frac{1}{6}$
(8) $\frac{1}{8}$

2
(1) $\frac{1}{2}$ (6) $\frac{1}{12}$
(2) $\frac{1}{2}$ (7) $\frac{2}{9}$
(3) $\frac{2}{5}$ (8) $\frac{3}{8}$
(4) $\frac{1}{4}$ (9) $\frac{5}{24}$
(5) $\frac{3}{5}$ (10) $\frac{5}{12}$

30 Multiplication of Fractions pp 60, 61

1
(1) $\frac{4}{5}\times2=\frac{4}{5}\times\frac{\boxed{2}}{1}$
   $=\frac{8}{5}=1\frac{3}{5}$
(2) $\frac{6}{7}$
(3) $1\frac{1}{8}$
(4) $\frac{8}{9}$
(5) $1\frac{1}{11}$

(6) $1\frac{4}{5}$
(7) $1\frac{1}{7}$
(8) $\frac{10}{13}$
(9) $\frac{12}{17}$
(10) $1\frac{1}{11}$

2
(1) $\frac{2}{5}$ (6) $1\frac{1}{4}$
(2) $\frac{5}{6}$ (7) $5\frac{1}{4}$
(3) $\frac{3}{7}$ (8) $3\frac{1}{3}$
(4) $\frac{4}{5}$ (9) $4\frac{1}{5}$
(5) $1\frac{2}{3}$ (10) $\frac{4}{7}$

31 Multiplication of Fractions pp 62, 63

1
(1) $1\frac{2}{5}\times\frac{3}{4}=\boxed{\frac{7}{5}}\times\frac{3}{4}=\frac{21}{20}=1\frac{1}{20}$
(2) $2\frac{1}{3}\times\frac{2}{5}=\frac{7}{3}\times\frac{2}{5}=\frac{14}{15}$
(3) $\frac{3}{4}\times2\frac{1}{7}=\frac{3}{4}\times\boxed{\frac{15}{7}}=\frac{45}{28}=1\frac{17}{28}$
(4) $5\frac{5}{6}$
(5) $3\frac{1}{30}$

(6) $2\frac{7}{24}$
(7) $3\frac{17}{45}$
(8) $1\frac{23}{42}$
(9) $5\frac{1}{4}$
(10) $9\frac{1}{7}$

2 (1) $2\frac{1}{3} \times \frac{3}{4} = \frac{7}{3} \times \frac{3}{4} = \frac{\boxed{7}}{4} = 1\frac{3}{4}$ (5) $3\frac{1}{7}$

(2) $1\frac{1}{2} \times \frac{4}{5} = \frac{3}{2} \times \frac{4}{5} = \frac{6}{5} = 1\frac{1}{5}$ (6) $\frac{11}{15}$

(3) $\frac{3}{4} \times 2\frac{2}{5} = \frac{3}{4} \times \frac{12}{5} = \frac{9}{5} = 1\frac{4}{5}$ (7) $5\frac{1}{2}$

(4) $3\frac{1}{2} \times 2\frac{1}{7} = \frac{7}{2} \times \frac{15}{7} = \frac{15}{2} = 7\frac{1}{2}$ (8) $10\frac{1}{2}$

(32) Multiplication of Fractions   pp 64,65

1 (1) $2\frac{1}{4} \times \frac{2}{3} = \frac{9}{4} \times \frac{2}{3}$ (5) $1\frac{1}{2} \times 1\frac{1}{3} = \frac{3}{2} \times \frac{4}{3}$

$= \frac{\boxed{3}}{2} = 1\frac{1}{2}$ $= 2$

(2) $3\frac{3}{4} \times \frac{2}{3} = \frac{15}{4} \times \frac{2}{3}$ (6) 2

$= \frac{5}{2} = 2\frac{1}{2}$

(3) $\frac{3}{5} \times 1\frac{2}{3} = \frac{3}{5} \times \frac{5}{3}$ (7) $2\frac{2}{5} \times 1\frac{7}{8} = \frac{12}{5} \times \frac{15}{8}$

$= 1$ $= \frac{9}{2} = 4\frac{1}{2}$

(4) 2 (8) $2\frac{1}{7} \times 3\frac{1}{9} = \frac{15}{7} \times \frac{28}{9}$

$= \frac{20}{3} = 6\frac{2}{3}$

2 (1) $\frac{8}{15}$ (6) $3\frac{1}{3}$

(2) $\frac{2}{3}$ (7) $\frac{3}{10}$

(3) $\frac{2}{3}$ (8) $\frac{5}{7}$

(4) $1\frac{1}{54}$ (9) 5

(5) $3\frac{3}{7}$ (10) $5\frac{5}{12}$

(33) Division of Fractions   pp 66,67

1 (1) $\frac{4}{5} \div \frac{3}{7} = \frac{4}{5} \times \frac{\boxed{7}}{\boxed{3}}$ (6) $2\frac{3}{16}$ **2** (1) $\frac{14}{15}$ (6) $1\frac{1}{14}$

$= \frac{28}{15} = 1\frac{13}{15}$ (2) $1\frac{7}{8}$ (7) $1\frac{1}{35}$

(2) $\frac{15}{28}$ (7) $\frac{16}{35}$ (3) $\frac{18}{35}$ (8) $1\frac{17}{63}$

(3) $\frac{18}{35}$ (8) $\frac{35}{36}$ (4) $\frac{3}{8}$ (9) $1\frac{13}{32}$

(4) $1\frac{17}{18}$ (9) $1\frac{1}{35}$ (5) $3\frac{1}{3}$ (10) $\frac{35}{48}$

(5) $1\frac{17}{18}$ (10) $\frac{18}{35}$

(34) Division of Fractions   pp 68,69

1 (1) $\frac{4}{5} \div \frac{2}{3} = \frac{4}{5} \times \frac{3}{2}$ (6) $1\frac{1}{4}$ **2** (1) $1\frac{1}{5}$ (6) $1\frac{1}{20}$

$= \frac{6}{5} = 1\frac{1}{5}$

(2) $1\frac{3}{4}$ (7) $1\frac{1}{14}$ (2) $\frac{5}{6}$ (7) $\frac{3}{8}$

(3) $1\frac{2}{5}$ (8) $\frac{2}{3}$ (3) $1\frac{1}{14}$ (8) $\frac{6}{7}$

(4) $2\frac{1}{3}$ (9) $\frac{7}{27}$ (4) $\frac{2}{5}$ (9) $\frac{44}{45}$

(5) $\frac{7}{10}$ (10) $\frac{9}{13}$ (5) $3\frac{1}{2}$ (10) $\frac{15}{28}$

(35) Division of Fractions   pp 70,71

1 (1) $\frac{1}{7} \div 2 = \frac{1}{7} \div \frac{2}{1} = \frac{1}{7} \times \frac{1}{2}$ (6) $3 \div \frac{1}{4} = \frac{3}{1} \times \frac{4}{1}$

$= \frac{1}{14}$ $= 12$

(2) $\frac{1}{12}$ (7) 2

(3) $\frac{2}{9}$ (8) $6\frac{2}{3}$

(4) $\frac{6}{35}$ (9) $8\frac{3}{4}$

(5) $\frac{3}{50}$ (10) $6\frac{2}{5}$

2 (1) $\frac{4}{7} \div 2 = \frac{4}{7} \times \frac{1}{2} = \frac{2}{7}$ (6) $3 \div \frac{3}{4} = \frac{3}{1} \times \frac{4}{3} = 4$

(2) $\frac{2}{7}$ (7) 9

(3) $\frac{2}{15}$ (8) $10\frac{1}{2}$

(4) $\frac{3}{20}$ (9) 18

(5) $\frac{3}{80}$ (10) $8\frac{4}{5}$

36 Division of Fractions pp72,73

1 (1) $\dfrac{8}{21} \div \dfrac{4}{7} = \dfrac{8}{21} \times \dfrac{7}{4} = \dfrac{2}{3}$ (5) $1\dfrac{1}{5}$

(2) $\dfrac{8}{21} \div \dfrac{2}{7} = \dfrac{8}{21} \times \dfrac{7}{2} = \dfrac{4}{3} = 1\dfrac{1}{3}$ (6) $\dfrac{2}{3}$

(3) $\dfrac{5}{12} \div \dfrac{5}{8} = \dfrac{5}{12} \times \dfrac{8}{5} = \dfrac{2}{3}$ (7) $\dfrac{5}{8}$

(4) $1\dfrac{1}{2}$ (8) $\dfrac{5}{6}$

2 (1) $\dfrac{9}{4} \div \dfrac{3}{8} = \dfrac{9}{4} \times \dfrac{8}{3} = 6$ (6) $\dfrac{2}{3}$

(2) 2 (7) $\dfrac{3}{4}$

(3) 4 (8) $\dfrac{5}{12}$

(4) $2\dfrac{2}{3}$ (9) $\dfrac{2}{9}$

(5) $2\dfrac{1}{4}$ (10) $\dfrac{5}{12}$

37 Division of Fractions pp74,75

1 (1) $1\dfrac{3}{4} \div \dfrac{2}{3} = \dfrac{7}{4} \div \dfrac{2}{3}$
$= \dfrac{7}{4} \times \dfrac{3}{2}$
$= \dfrac{21}{8} = 2\dfrac{5}{8}$

(6) $2\dfrac{3}{5} \div 1\dfrac{3}{4} = \dfrac{13}{5} \div \dfrac{7}{4}$
$= \dfrac{13}{5} \times \dfrac{4}{7}$
$= \dfrac{52}{35} = 1\dfrac{17}{35}$

(2) $2\dfrac{1}{10}$ (7) $2\dfrac{14}{15}$

(3) $1\dfrac{17}{28}$ (8) $5\dfrac{4}{9}$

(4) $1\dfrac{5}{8} \div 2\dfrac{1}{3} = \dfrac{13}{8} \div \dfrac{7}{3}$
$= \dfrac{13}{8} \times \dfrac{3}{7}$
$= \dfrac{39}{56}$

(9) $2\dfrac{1}{2} \div 3 = \dfrac{5}{2} \div \dfrac{3}{1}$
$= \dfrac{5}{2} \times \dfrac{1}{3}$
$= \dfrac{5}{6}$

(5) $\dfrac{9}{20}$ (10) $3\dfrac{8}{9}$

2 (1) $2\dfrac{1}{3} \div \dfrac{4}{9} = \dfrac{7}{3} \div \dfrac{4}{9}$
$= \dfrac{7}{3} \times \dfrac{9}{4}$
$= \dfrac{21}{4} = 5\dfrac{1}{4}$

(5) $\dfrac{2}{3} \div 1\dfrac{1}{6} = \dfrac{2}{3} \div \dfrac{7}{6}$
$= \dfrac{2}{3} \times \dfrac{6}{7}$
$= \dfrac{4}{7}$

(2) $2\dfrac{4}{7}$ (6) $\dfrac{8}{13}$

(3) $2\dfrac{1}{10}$ (7) $1\dfrac{1}{7}$

(4) $\dfrac{4}{5}$ (8) $2\dfrac{2}{15}$

38 Division of Fractions pp76,77

1 (1) $1\dfrac{1}{8} \div \dfrac{3}{4} = \dfrac{9}{8} \div \dfrac{3}{4}$
$= \dfrac{9}{8} \times \dfrac{4}{3}$
$= \dfrac{3}{2} = 1\dfrac{1}{2}$

(5) $\dfrac{1}{3}$

(2) $2\dfrac{2}{3}$ (6) $\dfrac{1}{6}$

(3) 2 (7) 2

(4) $2\dfrac{2}{5}$ (8) $\dfrac{2}{3}$

2 (1) $\dfrac{20}{21}$ (6) $9\dfrac{1}{3}$

(2) $2\dfrac{2}{9}$ (7) $2\dfrac{2}{3}$

(3) $\dfrac{5}{6}$ (8) $2\dfrac{1}{2}$

(4) $\dfrac{10}{21}$ (9) $\dfrac{11}{14}$

(5) $1\dfrac{1}{20}$ (10) $\dfrac{6}{7}$

39 Fractions and Decimals pp78,79

1 (1) $\dfrac{7}{5} = 7 \div 5 = 1.4$ (4) 0.03

(2) 0.125 (5) 2.43

(3) 7.75 (6) 0.027

2 (1) $0.6 = \dfrac{6}{10} = \dfrac{3}{5}$ (5) $1.2 = 1\dfrac{2}{10} = 1\dfrac{1}{5}$

(2) $0.05 = \dfrac{5}{100} = \dfrac{1}{20}$ (6) $2\dfrac{13}{25}$

(3) $0.18 = \dfrac{18}{100} = \dfrac{9}{50}$ (7) $3\dfrac{1}{8}$

(4) $0.032 = \dfrac{32}{1000} = \dfrac{4}{125}$ (8) $14\dfrac{1}{4}$

3 (1) $0.5 + \dfrac{1}{6} = \dfrac{1}{2} + \dfrac{1}{6}$
$= \dfrac{3}{6} + \dfrac{1}{6}$
$= \dfrac{4}{6} = \dfrac{2}{3}$

(6) $\dfrac{1}{2} - 0.3 = \dfrac{1}{2} - \dfrac{3}{10}$
$= \dfrac{5}{10} - \dfrac{3}{10}$
$= \dfrac{2}{10} = \dfrac{1}{5}$

(2) $0.2 + \dfrac{1}{4} = \dfrac{1}{5} + \dfrac{1}{4}$
$= \dfrac{4}{20} + \dfrac{5}{20}$
$= \dfrac{9}{20}$

(7) $\dfrac{1}{4} - 0.2 = \dfrac{1}{4} - \dfrac{1}{5}$
$= \dfrac{5}{20} - \dfrac{4}{20}$
$= \dfrac{1}{20}$

(3) $\dfrac{11}{12}$ (8) $\dfrac{1}{20}$

(4) $3\dfrac{1}{2} + 2.4 = 3\dfrac{1}{2} + 2\dfrac{2}{5}$
$= 3\dfrac{5}{10} + 2\dfrac{4}{10}$
$= 5\dfrac{9}{10}$

(9) $2\dfrac{1}{5} - 0.25 = 2\dfrac{1}{5} - \dfrac{1}{4}$
$= 2\dfrac{4}{20} - \dfrac{5}{20}$
$= 1\dfrac{24}{20} - \dfrac{5}{20}$
$= 1\dfrac{19}{20}$

(5) $1\dfrac{19}{30}$ (10) $2\dfrac{4}{15}$

40 Fractions and Decimals $\quad$ pp 80, 81

1 (1) $0.2 \times \dfrac{5}{6} = \dfrac{\boxed{1}}{5} \times \dfrac{5}{6} = \dfrac{1}{6}$ $\qquad$ (6) $\dfrac{5}{28} \times 0.7 = \dfrac{5}{28} \times \dfrac{7}{10} = \dfrac{1}{8}$

(2) $\dfrac{2}{5}$ $\qquad$ (7) $8\dfrac{3}{4}$

(3) $\dfrac{2}{35}$ $\qquad$ (8) 2

(4) $0.25 \times 3\dfrac{1}{5} = \dfrac{\boxed{1}}{4} \times \dfrac{\boxed{16}}{5} = \dfrac{4}{5}$ $\quad$ (9) 12

(5) $0.15 \times 40 = \dfrac{\boxed{3}}{20} \times \dfrac{\boxed{40}}{1} = 6$ $\qquad$ (10) $\dfrac{1}{3}$

2 (1) $0.6 \div \dfrac{2}{3} = \dfrac{3}{5} \div \dfrac{2}{3}$ $\qquad$ (6) $1\dfrac{2}{3} \div 0.5 = \dfrac{5}{3} \div \dfrac{1}{2}$

$\qquad\quad = \dfrac{3}{5} \times \dfrac{3}{2}$ $\qquad\qquad\qquad = \dfrac{5}{3} \times \dfrac{2}{1}$

$\qquad\quad = \dfrac{9}{10}$ $\qquad\qquad\qquad\quad = \dfrac{10}{3} = 3\dfrac{1}{3}$

(2) $1\dfrac{1}{5}$ $\qquad$ (7) $\dfrac{1}{2}$

(3) $2\dfrac{7}{10}$ $\qquad$ (8) 5

(4) 1 $\qquad$ (9) 25

(5) $1.25 \div \dfrac{5}{6} = \dfrac{5}{4} \times \dfrac{6}{5}$ $\qquad$ (10) 3

$\qquad\quad = \dfrac{3}{2} = 1\dfrac{1}{2}$

41 Three Fractions $\quad$ pp 82, 83

1 (1) $\dfrac{3}{4} \times \dfrac{2}{5} \times \dfrac{5}{9} = \dfrac{3 \times 2 \times 5}{4 \times 5 \times 9}$ $\quad$ (6) $\dfrac{1}{14}$

$\qquad\qquad\qquad\quad = \dfrac{\boxed{1}}{6}$

(2) $\dfrac{2}{15}$ $\qquad$ (7) $\dfrac{1}{12}$

(3) 12 $\qquad$ (8) $\dfrac{5}{14}$

(4) $\dfrac{4}{21}$ $\qquad$ (9) $\dfrac{2}{5}$

(5) $\dfrac{1}{4}$ $\qquad$ (10) $\dfrac{1}{4}$

2 (1) $\dfrac{5}{8}$ $\qquad$ (6) $\dfrac{1}{2}$

(2) $1\dfrac{2}{3}$ $\qquad$ (7) $\dfrac{1}{2}$

(3) 1 $\qquad$ (8) $\dfrac{1}{14}$

(4) $\dfrac{1}{3}$ $\qquad$ (9) $\dfrac{4}{7}$

(5) $\dfrac{8}{15}$ $\qquad$ (10) $1\dfrac{2}{5}$

42 Three Numbers $\;\blacklozenge$Mixed Calculations $\quad$ pp 84, 85

1 (1) $4 \div \dfrac{2}{3} \div 2 = \dfrac{4}{1} \times \dfrac{3}{\boxed{2}} \times \dfrac{\boxed{1}}{2} = 3$ $\qquad$ (6) 1

(2) 12 $\qquad$ (7) $\dfrac{1}{10}$

(3) $2\dfrac{2}{5}$ $\qquad$ (8) $\dfrac{1}{10}$

(4) $2\dfrac{1}{12}$ $\qquad$ (9) $3\dfrac{1}{3}$

(5) $\dfrac{2}{3}$ $\qquad$ (10) $3\dfrac{1}{3}$

2 (1) $\dfrac{3}{4} \times \dfrac{3}{5} \div 0.2 = \dfrac{3}{4} \times \dfrac{3}{5} \times \dfrac{5}{1} = \dfrac{9}{4} = 2\dfrac{1}{4}$ $\quad$ (6) $\dfrac{1}{5}$

(2) $2\dfrac{1}{2}$ $\qquad$ (7) $\dfrac{3}{25}$

(3) $\dfrac{1}{6}$ $\qquad$ (8) $1\dfrac{7}{9}$

(4) $\dfrac{1}{2}$ $\qquad$ (9) $\dfrac{25}{42}$

(5) $\dfrac{1}{4}$ $\qquad$ (10) $\dfrac{2}{3}$

43 Review $\quad$ pp 86, 87

1 (1) $\dfrac{5}{7}$ $\quad$ (3) $\dfrac{1}{3}$ $\quad$ (5) $\dfrac{4}{9}$ $\qquad$ **3** (1) $\dfrac{3}{8}$ $\quad$ (3) $1\dfrac{1}{4}$

$\quad$ (2) $\dfrac{3}{5}$ $\quad$ (4) $\dfrac{5}{6}$ $\quad$ (6) $\dfrac{1}{3}$ $\qquad$ (2) $\dfrac{11}{15}$ $\quad$ (4) $\dfrac{1}{2}$

2 (1) $\dfrac{11}{15}$ $\quad$ (5) $1\dfrac{1}{20}$ $\qquad$ **4** (1) $\dfrac{8}{21}$ $\quad$ (4) $\dfrac{9}{20}$

$\quad$ (2) $\dfrac{19}{24}$ $\quad$ (6) $2\dfrac{1}{2}$ $\qquad$ (2) $\dfrac{1}{2}$ $\quad$ (5) $1\dfrac{1}{5}$

$\quad$ (3) $\dfrac{1}{2}$ $\quad$ (7) $2\dfrac{31}{36}$ $\qquad$ (3) $4\dfrac{2}{3}$ $\quad$ (6) $1\dfrac{2}{3}$

$\quad$ (4) $1\dfrac{9}{10}$ $\quad$ (8) $4\dfrac{8}{15}$ $\qquad$ **5** (1) $1\dfrac{1}{4}$ $\quad$ (4) 10

$\qquad\qquad\qquad\qquad\qquad\qquad\quad$ (2) $1\dfrac{5}{27}$ $\quad$ (5) $1\dfrac{22}{27}$

$\qquad\qquad\qquad\qquad\qquad\qquad\quad$ (3) $\dfrac{2}{7}$ $\quad$ (6) $1\dfrac{1}{5}$

Advice

If you made a mistake in **1**, start reviewing on page 8.

If you made a mistake in **2**, start reviewing on page 20.

If you made a mistake in **3**, start reviewing on page 40.

If you made a mistake in **4**, start reviewing on page 54.

If you made a mistake in **5**, start reviewing on page 66.